The Very Latest E-Mini Trading

2nd Edition

The Very Latest E-Mini Trading

*Using Market Anticipation
to Trade Electronic Futures*

2nd Edition

Michael J. Gutmann

ISBN 1-4528-8932-5

Trading the financial markets has large potential rewards, but also large potential risk. You must be aware of the risks and be willing to accept them in order to invest in the stock, futures and options markets. Don't trade with money you can't afford to lose. This material is neither a solicitation nor an offer to buy or sell stocks, futures or options. No representation is being made that any account will or is likely to achieve profits or losses similar to those discussed in this book. The individual trades described in this book include both hypothetical positions used to illustrate a general trading technique and actual trades. The past performance of any trading system or methodology is not necessarily indicative of future results.

Library of Congress Cataloging-in-Publication Data

Gutmann, Michael J.
    The very latest e-mini trading : using market anticipation to trade electronic futures, 2nd edition / by Michael J. Gutmann

    Includes index.

    ISBN 1-4528-8932-5

    1. Trading and investing. 2. Day trading. 3. Electronic trading. 4. Futures. 5. E-Mini. 6. 2nd Edition. I. Title.

To the memory of my father
Helmut R. Gutmann,
and to my mother
Elizabeth M. Gutmann.
They set an example of hard work and
were dedicated to intellectual pursuits.
I am always grateful.

Acknowledgments

I want to thank the many traders, novice and experienced, who purchased the first edition of the book.

One of the joys of authoring a trading text such as this is that it facilitates meeting and corresponding with other traders. I have received many compliments on the first edition and, importantly, been given insightful comments and suggestions that have improved my trading and writing about trading immensely. To everyone with whom I've corresponded and spoken regarding the e-minis, a big Thank You – for your contributions and support!

Once again, I must thank my wife, Sandy, for giving me free rein to pursue my trading efforts and the time to write this book, now twice over.

Acknowledgments (from the 1st Edition)

I have many people to thank for their help and support, and with this book in particular.

Ravi Vedanayagam has been an Intel colleague, business partner and close friend for more than 20 years. Together we attempted to master the art of trading. It has been a memorable experience, to say the least. Ravi's humor, support and encouragement have been invaluable.

I became acquainted with Dr. Humphrey E.D. Lloyd after reading his charming autobiography, <u>While Memory Serves</u>, several years ago, and he has been a good friend and colleague ever since. Dr. Lloyd has had two successful careers, first as prominent physician and then as investor and trader. In the latter instance he has written several texts and is a member of the American Association of Professional Technical Analysts. Humphrey first reviewed the book's manuscript and gave excellent detailed comments and uncovered numerous errata. It was with his help that I completed the work.

Chet Hearn, a friend of Humphrey's, and to whom I still owe some TradeStation code, I might add, has been someone to exchange trading ideas with over the last couple of years.

Peter Bennett and I studied math together at the University of Minnesota and have been friends for more than 30 years. Peter's encouragement and intelligence have helped keep me motivated. Todd Kimball, a good friend from a local Toastmaster's Club, was uniquely inspirational.

Much of my professional career was spent at Intel and I want to thank colleagues and friends there. This includes Vijay Rao and Kamal Shah; Ramesh Illikkal and Hani El-Gebaly; along with Stephen, Emily, Sankar, Pratyush, and others from the old Intel VideoPhone gang; and going even further back, N. Kumar and N. Bhasker. Two memorable bosses at Intel were Sanjay Panditji, who first hired me, and Taymoor Arshi, who gave me an early role on the ProShare team. George Dallas, another Intel colleague and now a serious trader, was encouraging when reviewing my trading activities.

The "Third Avenue Book Club," Gerry, Alison, Greg, Carol, Bob, Lynn, Sandy, and I, have been meeting regularly now for some 14 years, even as our book-of-the-month selection has been replaced with dinners and lots of wine. They are a special source of camaraderie.

Jeff Eizenberg at Attain Capital is a helpful industry contact who offered suggestions with some of my early attempts writing about trading. The team at Futures Magazine, Daniel Collins, James Holter, and Christine Birkner, gave me the opportunity to publish early articles about trading e-mini futures. Christine expertly edited my early writings.

Raymond Deux, NinjaTrader CEO, was kind enough to forward an early version of the book to Josh Peng, NinjaTrader Certified Expert, for a review, which helped with the descriptions of NinjaTrader.

Teresa Lo, a veteran trader, investment advisor and founder of InVivo Analytics, as well as the inventor of the InVivo.Stops described in the book, provided comments on the manuscript and earlier helped me understand the InVivo.Stops logic.

Steve Eberbach, a knowledgeable and expert developer of novel trading strategies, gave the manuscript a thorough review. Steve found numerous errata and greatly improved the quality of the book.

Garry Zamberlan found errors in some original trade strategy expected value calculations and we worked remotely to make the needed corrections. Garry's help is greatly appreciated.

Vivek Chetty worked one summer with Ravi and me developing tools for an options writing program and testing e-mini futures trading. He quickly recognized the importance of market anticipation when day-trading. I certainly benefited from Vivek's insight.

My family is my greatest source of inspiration and support. My parents, Helmut and Elizabeth Gutmann, worked tirelessly to raise me and give me the tools needed to be successful in life. My brother David and older sister, Ruth, have been supportive siblings, commending me on my entrepreneurial efforts. My younger sister, Rebecca, takes my many phone calls and offers intelligent humor and support.

My son, Danny, taught me Texas Hold 'em and together we discuss the similarities of gambling and trading. Danny provided welcome relief from the trading desk, even if it meant that he repeatedly beat me at ping pong. My daughter, Marla, inspires me with her joy, music-making and her academic ambitions; and I appreciate her not-so-subtle skepticism when it comes to the trading endeavor.

Sandy, my wife of 28 years, has given me the greatest gift of all – her unconditional love. Sandy is a wonderfully kind partner, and she is particularly encouraging with my writing.

To those friends and colleagues whom I have mistakenly omitted – my sincere apologies. I thank you all!

Table of Contents

The Very Latest E-Mini Trading

2nd Edition

Preface to the 2nd Edition

After writing a trading text it becomes crystal clear how quickly the trading endeavor changes. Not only does one's trading style continually evolve, but so do the financial markets. Nothing ever sits still in this business for too long.

While I was fairly satisfied with the original version of <u>The Very Latest E-Mini Trading</u>, I also wanted to keep the material up-to-date and to include the latest techniques I had learned and developed. I enjoy writing about trading and this 2nd Edition naturally followed the original text.

In most every case, the material in this edition is entirely additive. The trader gets additional views of the market and trading techniques, not a re-dress of the original.

In order to assist readers of the original text, what will be referred to as the 1st Edition, let me outline the specific additions that are part of the 2nd Edition.

CME Data Feed Change Requires Tick Chart Interval Modifications. Shortly after the 1st Edition went to press (July 2009), the CME made a change in its trade reporting. From the CME website:

> "… trades are now reported … at a much more granular level. Previously, data from a trade event involving multiple orders at the same price were reported mostly in two data blocks. Now, trade events are reported with greater granularity. For a single trade event, a trade data block will be sent for each resting order. This provides customers with better visibility into market activity."

Apparently the CME went from coalescing trades that completed at the same price to breaking out trades based on individual resting limit orders – limit orders that are submitted ahead of the market and are to fill only at a pre-defined price. (Much more will be said about resting limit orders and electronic order matching later in the book.) The result of this change was that some of the 233-tick charts used earlier produced too many bars. Many traders found that decreasing tick bar frequency by two or three times gave them the kind of tick charts they had been accustomed to before the CME change. I was no different.

In order to manage the additional data, the S&P 500 e-mini, ES, has been moved to 764-tick charts; the Nasdaq-100 e-mini, NQ, to 382-tick charts (twice the ES frequency); while the DJIA e-mini, YM, and Russell 2000 small-cap e-mini, TF, remain at their original 233-tick intervals.

Because of these changes, one naturally might be skeptical of the practice of using tick charts. If a subtle change in exchange trade reporting can make for radically different chart settings, then can tick charts be relied on?

Tick charts are useful because they are responsive to increased market activity. In this sense they allow the trader to "look inside" fixed time-interval bars to get a better idea of the trading taking place. Often technical indicators appear more responsive with tick charts. The down-side to tick charts is that they obscure time. For example, when the market is inactive, there can be fewer bars shown than in the fixed time interval case. More will be said about the use of tick charts later in the book.

Use of Statistical Technical Indicators. The 1st Edition made many references to the MACD technical indicator. The MACD continues to be a widely used indicator even though introduced some 50 years ago.

MACD output is relative to the underlying asset. That is, if used with a stock, then its signals might be based on some number of cents; if used with a futures contract, then its signals might be based on some number of ticks. So moving the MACD from asset to asset requires adjustment in the interpretation of its output. This can be tedious and error-prone.

The 1st Edition of the book contained tables of MACD overbought and oversold settings that varied across the four key e-minis that make up the trading system. I grew tired of this and looked for a more robust version of the MACD.

As a result, a technique of moving the MACD software (and other similar indicators) to statistical outputs was developed. Specifically, instead of underlying prices, the new Statistical MACD outputs *z-score* values, where a z-score is a number of standard deviations a current value is from a mean value. Now, instead of saying the overbought setting is 1.5 points for the ES contract (S&P 500 e-mini) and 0.7 points for the TF contract (Russell 2000 e-mini), a number of standard deviations are referenced. For example, the MACD can be considered overbought or oversold at plus or minus two standard deviations. This seems like a useful simplification. The 2nd Edition also covers a new price extension indicator (APR SD) that is similarly statistical.

Specific Price Patterns Added to Trade Setups. This is perhaps the biggest addition to the 1st Edition.

The original trading system was based on four key views of the market:

1. Day-Type – Is the day trending or rotational.
2. Price Level – Can a pre-defined price level be found and used to trade.
3. Technical Indication of Price Extension – When fading the market, the MACD was used to assist in determining if price was over-extended and therefore due for a possible reversal.
4. Time-of-Day – Knowledge of certain time-of-day trading patterns in the stock market that help the day-trader navigate the trading session. For example, the first hour of the day session creates a trading range against which trades can be placed.

From these views of the market, specific trade setups were defined. This part of the trading system is unchanged and continues to be central to it.

I have experimented with, and now regularly use, some very specific price patterns that take some of the guess work out of discretionary trade decisions. Many of these are extremely well-known and were covered in the 1st Edition. For example, 20-EMA retracements, making use of double-bottoms, and viewing a third time up test failure as a trade opportunity. Specifying detailed price patterns as a part of trade setups makes the system less ambiguous.

The 2nd Edition includes a number of very specific price patterns that are added to the four trading views. In some sense, the price patterns add a fifth leg to the system. Do they finally complete the puzzle and make for a 100% complete system? Time will tell. Given the evolutionary aspect of the trading endeavor, I suspect there will never be a "final-final" system.

A new chapter has been added to the book to cover price patterns used for trade entries. In some cases, trade setup details from the 1st Edition have been re-organized to improve the flow of the book.

Incorporation of Stop Market Orders. The 1st Edition of the book advocated the use of Limit orders to place new resting Bids (Longs) and Asks (Shorts) in the market. There were a number of reasons for this approach, but essentially it was to encourage trading that required fore-thought and planning as opposed to emotionally chasing price with Market orders. My trading was both more profitable with Limit orders and I came away, even from losing trades, with a sense the trading had been executed to a plan when Limit orders were used.

But I also recognize that there are good breakout setups that can make use of Stop Market orders and there are many traders, myself included, who want the option to enter the market as it moves in the direction of a trade setup. It can be difficult to set a resting limit order in a fast moving and volatile market, especially after having been run over a few times in failed trades.

In fact, Stop Market orders, as they are used in the 2nd Edition, can adhere to the anticipation goal of the trading system if they are placed ahead of the market in the same manner as a Limit order. If there are valid setups where a pre-defined Stop Market order can be used and set ahead, then there is no reason to categorically eliminate them. Some of the new price patterns introduced in this edition make use of Stop Market entry orders.

Additional Market Profile Based Trades. The 1st Edition trading system relied on Market Profile theory quite extensively, but did not include a number of well-known Market Profile based trades, primarily those that use the Value Area. These are now widely used by the day-trading community. Additional Market Profile trades are included in this edition so that the book is more complete.

There is a tendency, when writing a follow-on edition such as this, to include too much new material. One has a baseline to work with – the previous edition – and it can be compared to what has recently been written in the subject area. Then the author may feel compelled to add material so that the new edition covers more and more ground. However, in doing so, the work can lose focus and become a collection of well-known ideas and practices, as opposed to an original contribution.

To address this issue, I have included new material only when it covers techniques that I make use of in my own trading – nothing more and nothing less. Where I have wanted to point out material that I think the reader might be interested in generally, but which is outside the scope of the current trading techniques, I have made a note in the text or as a footnote.

Finally, the 2nd Edition corrects all known errata from the 1st Edition and includes numerous stylistic updates.

Many thanks to all the readers of the 1st Edition – especially for your comments and support.

§§§

Introduction

Is E-Mini Day-Trading For Real?

I never imagined I would write this book. I never imagined I'd be day-trading the electronic futures market. And I never imagined I'd be advocating doing so in a how-to book.

I've learned a means of trading electronic futures that offers the possibility of regular income with low risk. To be able to successfully trade this way requires developing unique approaches and techniques.

Before getting too far ahead, let's look at the kind of results the trading techniques described in this book can deliver. An actual trading snapshot from a recent week of live trading one to three mini-sized electronic futures contracts, referred to as e-minis, gave the following results:

Performance	All Trades	Long Trades	Short Trades
Start Date	1/5/2009		
End Date	1/9/2009		
Total Net Profit	1580.00	915.00	665.00
Gross Profit	3032.50	1002.50	2030.00
Gross Loss	-1452.50	-87.50	-1365.00
Commissions	544.00	92.00	452.00
Total Net Commissions	**1036.00**	823.00	213.00
Percent Profitable	70.59%	86.96%	67.26%
Max. conseq. Winners	11	10	9
Max. conseq. Losers	3	1	3
Largest Winning Trade	0.52%	0.52%	0.42%
Largest Losing Trade	-0.37%	-0.13%	-0.37%

These figures are actual live trading account results. The bottom-line is an account profit of approximately $1000 for the week.

There are futures brokers that require as little as $500 of margin per e-mini contract when day-trading. Other practitioners recommend up to $10,000 in margin per e-mini contract in order to tolerate and recover from account draw-downs. A middle-of-the-road margin figure is then $5000 per e-mini contract. The trading that produced these results used at most three e-mini contracts at any time for a total margin requirement of $15,000. The returns for the week shown here then represent a 6.6% return[1].

Because of the vast liquidity of the e-mini futures market and the tools used to execute the trading program described here, this kind of trading scales simply by increasing the e-mini contract quantity values set in PC trading software – up to the account size and psychology the trader can bear, of course. More about this will be covered in the chapters that follow.

Provided these results can be replicated the potential for this system is quite spectacular.

What type of trading generated that week's result? Again, before taking the reader too far down the path, let's take a quick look at the type of trading the system described in this book uses.

Most of the trades require setting a trade entry ahead of the market. A specific price point is anticipated to be at a level where the market has a good possibility of reversing or extending its course. If the expected price action occurs, a winning position is likely, provided correct trade management is used. To this end, once in the trade, software automation moves the trader quickly to a no-lose, on-the-house position, from where a "winning runner" trade might develop. The same software automation is used to protect the trader, should the market not make a turn in his or her favor. A couple of examples illustrate the technique.

The first chart below shows a trade which did not result in a winning runner. A "resting limit order" was placed at the "Initial Balance High" price level. The order was filled and software automation quickly hit fast exit profit targets. From this point on the trader is in a no-lose, on-the-house position. The trade eventually closed with automated stop-loss,

---

[1] A good week of trading.

but it was considered successful nonetheless, because it put the trader in a no-lose, on-the-house position with the possibility of a larger winner.

The second chart below shows a trade which resulted in a good winning runner. Again, a resting limit order was used, this time at the "Day's Previous High" price level. The order was filled and software automation quickly hit fast exit profit targets. The trade then developed a sizeable winning runner of more than six ES (e-mini S&P 500 futures contract) points, which is considered an excellent result by any practicing e-mini day-trader.

A major theme of the trading system is:

- Anticipate the market using pre-defined price levels and price patterns.
- Enter trades with pre-set orders that are ahead of the market.
- Apply software automation to quickly take fast profits on some fraction of the original position.
- Attempt to achieve a winning runner on the remainder of the position.
- Software automation is always used to enter and exit the market and protects the trader with stop-loss.

Determining how and when the market can be anticipated and how and when to employ software automation is the subject of this book.

There is a great sense of accomplishment in dueling successfully with the sharp knife that is the electronic futures market. When analytical techniques are combined with the inherent thrill of trading, it becomes one of the most compelling and rewarding endeavors I know.

Because I enjoy writing about trade techniques and trading, this book is a natural outcome of the last several years of my trading experience.

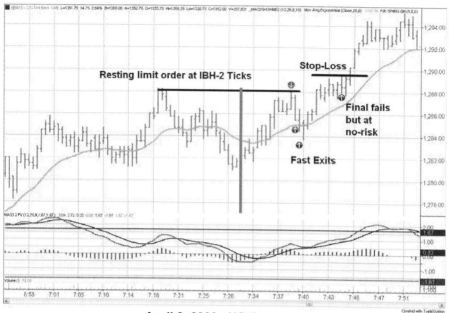

April 2, 2009. NQ Contract

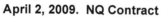

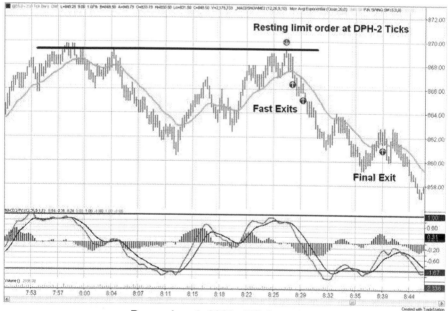

December 4, 2008. ES Contract

Past to Present

When writing that I never imagined I'd be day-trading electronic futures I meant it. My father, who this year (2009) would have celebrated his 98th birthday, was a physician and chemist with a long career in basic cancer research, publishing over 100 articles in the most prestigious journals in the field. His study at home had a large bookshelf covering one wall. He was devoted to science. My mother, who this year will celebrate her 89th birthday, worked on a doctorate in entomology. I came from a home where education and intellectual achievement were a priority. My father's hero was Einstein. On the weekend we played violin duets together.

I studied math at the University of Minnesota and at first toyed with the idea of becoming a professional mathematician. In my last year, I did a senior project with a fairly prominent Hungarian mathematician. In his office one day he said, "Looking at the big picture, while you can get a PhD in mathematics, I think you'll make for one more mediocre mathematician. But you can be a good engineer. Why don't you think about that?" (In my own defense, I continue to imagine his standards were high.) The next day I walked over to the school of engineering to inquire about graduate school.

I spent 25 years in the computer industry as a programmer and a manager of programmers. Twenty of those years were at Intel, where I was lucky to land a job and worked hard to be successful. Being a software engineer, I didn't learn how to design microprocessors but I did become an expert programmer. This was the advent of the PC revolution and Intel and Microsoft were at the heart of it. I was fortunate to work along-side talented engineers on good projects. This included a large operating system and a novel video conferencing system. Perhaps the highlight of my career was as a project manager on the Intel VideoPhone.

Growing up I would watch Wall Street Week with Louis Rukeyser. I think I cultivated an interest in Wall Street to distinguish myself from my parents, who seemed uninterested in money if it ever became too much of a focus. In high-school, I sometimes paper-traded stocks. At Intel, unlike the more academic environment I'd grown up in, it was all about money – margins, quarterly profits, market share. There were lucrative employee stock participation and stock option programs. As Intel grew, I became interested in how to best make use of my small bit of new stock option wealth. (Based on a current 2009 stock price, when I joined the company in 1983 Intel shares were trading around $0.40. By 2000 they would reach an all-time high of over $75.00.) I began lightly trading stock and stock options using a local broker. And then came the tech bubble.

In the late 90's Intel employees were always talking about buying high-tech stocks, even if in fact they were just holding Intel shares collected through employee stock purchase and option grant programs. But as the tech phenomenon exploded, people at work, like everywhere else, seemed to be making serious money investing in high-tech.

At the beginning of November 1999, I bought shares in a new tech stock, Red Hat. Red Hat was going to sell the increasingly popular Linux operating system which had the potential of competing with Microsoft Windows. On November 1st, the stock was around $45 a share, which is where I bought it. By the end of the month it had risen to $125. I couldn't believe it. I bought a Mazda Miata roadster and paid cash. I remember bragging about my Red Hat trade. Some of us at work would joke pretentiously, "In this market, if you can't make $50,000 by lunch time you're an idiot."

More important than the Red Hat trade was a realization that with a modest amount of capital it was possible to make serious money that could equal or beat an Intel salary. For better or worse, this was a real eye-opener for me.

We all worked very hard at Intel. Business began at 8:00am every day, sometimes earlier. Often I did not arrive home in the evening until well after dinner. Weekends typically included at least a Saturday or Sunday in the office. The work was compelling and we were well-compensated, but to equal a year's salary in a matter of days or weeks speculating in the stock market made me question my employment and the entire work equation. Shouldn't I be able to leverage some of my savings and make the equivalent of an engineer's salary without the long hours and sweat that were Intel? In my spare time I began to seriously study techniques for making a regular income from the stock market.

Trying to pick individual stocks seemed problematic to me. I was not confident or patient enough to wait for a stock to appreciate over time, and while there was Red Hat, I also remember buying Sun Microsystems near its high and losing a significant amount of money when it crashed with the rest of the high-tech flyers in 2000. (I didn't typically use pre-set stop-loss orders at the time – everything just seemed to be going up.) Because I've loved math since college and I was an engineer, I thought I could bring some technical prowess to speculation beyond merely picking stocks. After reading several books I was determined to trade stock options as a means of replacing my Intel salary.

I paper-traded Covered Calls (collecting premium income from selling Call options on shares already owned) and covered short strangles (collecting premium income from selling Call and Put options while protecting the short positions with offsetting long option positions) on individual stocks. After several months of profitability, and following an unpleasant re-organization at work, I was even more determined to leave and strike out on my own.

By now I'd profitably paper-trading some options writing strategies for six months. One aspect to working for Intel, which pretty much every engineer I knew had come to accept, was that making the grade left very little time for anything else. An engineering career at Intel was great, but it came with an opportunity cost because Intel was all-consuming. After some 20 years, I got to feel that if I was ever going to do anything else it would require a break from the company, at least temporarily.

About this time, I heard a radio program that caught my attention. The show's guest was discussing a survey of men in middle-age who were asked what three aspects of their life they would change if given the chance. The answers apparently were consistent: (1) Take more risk; (2) Spend more time with family and friends; (3) Spend more time in reflection/prayer/meditation. After 20 years at Intel, I began feeling dated, and the first answer definitely got to me, especially when the dynamic high-tech sector could make a veteran feel stuck, like an old lamp post. Had I taken enough risk in my career? Would I have regrets?

I discussed leaving Intel with everyone and all the time. This included my family and friends, a physician, a Lutheran pastor. Basically, I got two responses. The first was: You have a good job at a great company, why do you want to rock the boat? You don't really know how to make money trading stocks and you still have two kids to put through college. You're crazy to leave! The second was: It's kind of a "no-brainer." You have some financial resources, but not enough to simply retire. Go see what you can do with it!

After a second difficult re-organization at work, I left Intel in the Spring of 2003. I immediately began to trade stock options in earnest.

I put up a website (thehumbletrader.com) and began documenting my trades and trading results. I wanted to be completely above-board, and I was determined to make use of everything I'd learned at Intel about project management and the discipline of engineering to be successful. I had some good early winning trades as well as some losing ones, as might be expected.

I have been seriously trading ever since.

§§§

E-Mini Futures Day-Trading

It's been written by a well-known trading psychologist[2] that there is no single trading personality – trading is not a monolithic exercise that either does or does not suit an individual. Rather, trading has enough variation to it that being successful means finding a niche that matches your personality.

I have found e-mini stock index futures trading to be an excellent niche, and this book is about how to day-trade e-mini futures. It's about a specific set of trading techniques and tools, as well as the psychology needed to execute them.

The novice trader repeatedly hears about trade psychology and is rightfully skeptical. It is difficult to accept that conquering the psychological aspects of trading may be the hardest part of all. For, we ask egotistically, What is there about my present make-up that can prevent me from making money?

Overcoming the psychological aspects of trading is the hardest part for me. Until one has learned to stop chasing markets, "getting short-in-the-hole," making up chart patterns that seemingly must be traded, trading at the wrong time of day, shorting rallies early, and other similar trading errors, it is not possible to make money. It takes time to learn how to recover from losing trades and to keep one's account from slowly draining away.

I enjoy writing and that includes writing notes and annotating charts every day about trades made and what I've learned from them. Much of this book is a careful collection and presentation from a trading log that spans several years. I came to the conclusion that I had something unique and maybe even important to record (of course, the reader will have to draw his or her own conclusions!) when the trading notes started to appear as:

> CTs Equivocal → Fade Wide IB. MACD-Price Divergence setup
> at IB High with 20-EMA Retracement Entry

and contained significant, non-trivial information with a consistency and repeatability to them. Now, to me, the above statement is entirely clear

---

[2] See Enhancing Trader Performance, Brett Steenbarger, John Wiley & Sons, 2007.

and makes good trading sense. And when I review it with an eye to the uninitiated, I've become convinced there is something to write about.

I decided to write this book knowing that with the vast scope of the e-mini futures market, even if a thousand retail traders started to practice my techniques exactly, I could continue to use them.

Here I have to give a standard note of caution. While I whole-heartedly believe in the techniques described in the text, trading is about practice, practice, practice. It's similar to learning a musical instrument or a skill sport, like tennis. Repetition of correct technique is key. Start with simulated trading; trade a small number of contracts with real money; initially work to keep your account at break even; and then proceed to profitability. Plan on making hundreds of trades before becoming proficient.

The next chapter, "The Road to the E-Mini," gives an overview of the stock and futures markets. The reader will want to know, Why the e-mini futures and why discretionary day-trading? This section of the book gives the background to help answer those questions. Readers interested in an introduction to a variety of markets and techniques will find a chronological overview of what I discovered as a trader. The scope of the retail trading "ecosystem" can be overwhelming to the new participant – all the available markets and techniques used to trade – and I hope this section will help others navigate trading for the first time. The experienced trader may wish to skip this chapter.

Chapter "Trading Basics" covers material needed to understand the trading system advocated in the book. Here the reader will learn some Market Profile theory, Price Level definition, Time-of-Day and Price Action considerations, and other trading basics. These are covered independently from the specific trade setups and execution details found in the next chapters.

Chapter "Price Patterns" describes specific price action patterns that aid the trader when taking positions. Price patterns help to make trade entry decisions less ambiguous.

Chapter "Trade Setups" describes the specific trades used by the e-mini stock index futures trading system. The setups draw from a combination of market views: Day-Type; Market Price Levels; Technical Indication; Time-of-Day and Price Patterns. It is by combining a number of independent inputs that the trades achieve a higher probability of success. The challenge is to organize and present the trade setups so that they are straightforward to use and repeatable in their application.

Chapter "Trade Management" covers the important aspect of how to enter a trade and then, once in a position, protect one's account with stop-loss orders and take profits with profit-target orders. Some newly developed tools and techniques are put to use to automate trade execution. Good trade management is sometimes over-looked but can make or break the trader.

Chapter "Trade Examples, Do's and Don'ts, Psychology" gives additional trade examples and guidelines that augment the trades described in the earlier chapters. It includes a number of do's and don'ts – common errors to avoid and trade setups to exploit. Additional trade psychology notes are included in this chapter.

Chapter "Final Thoughts" summarizes and concludes the book.

An excellent e-mini day-trader[3] once said, "It's the hardest way I know to make an easy buck." I couldn't agree more. Trading the e-mini futures has the potential of being both financially and personally rewarding, and justifying, to a large extent, all the blood, sweat and tears it takes to become successful at it.

§§§

---

[3] Visit www.jpjtrading.com if interested in a top-notch practitioner of Market Profile-based e-mini day-trading.

The Road to the E-Mini

[This chapter is a review of the author's evolution from stocks to stock options, stock index options, futures and futures options, including experience with automated system trading. It describes details of the e-mini stock index futures market and how and why day-trading e-mini stock index futures is a preferred trading vehicle. Experienced traders and/or those wishing to cut to the chase and begin reading about the E-Mini Futures Trading System may want to skip to the next chapter.]

When trading seriously, full- or part-time, the practitioner quickly faces questions of what trading style and market to use. Whatever technique is employed, he or she will undoubtedly run into losing trades, which naturally forces one to look for improvements in trading methodology and/or markets traded.

With the current diversity of techniques and markets, and all the media surrounding the endeavor ("Make millions trading Forex", "Use a mechanical system and take the emotion out of trading", etc.) figuring out techniques and markets that will lead to profitability is no mean feat. For the individual trader, the trading ecosystem is overwhelming, and until one has matured beyond looking endlessly for the trading Holy Grail, it's hard to trade comfortably on a regular basis.

In my case, it took several years to become comfortable with the various trading methods and markets in order to trade regularly with some confidence. While remaining generally curious, I no longer hope to find a trading Holy Grail around the next corner, waiting to be uncovered if only I will keep looking. Now, while my trading continues to improve, it does so incrementally. Becoming comfortable trading is knowing enough about the various markets and trading methods in practice, feeling one has made a good choice in the trading he or she is using, and that something important hasn't been over-looked.

The next sections give an overview of the key markets and popular trading techniques I found on the way to the e-mini stock index futures.

Stocks

For me, and I think it's pretty much true generally, speculation begins with the stock market. Historically, the stock market was the first market advertised for wide-spread public speculation, and Wall Street has played a colorful and important role in the history of American capitalism (notorious would be a better choice of words after the 2008-09 financial crisis). In my ninth grade social studies class we studied Wall Street and paper-traded stocks using the local newspaper's business section. Buying stocks on a hunch, at-the-market, and without any stop-loss or profit-targets was how I began.

Some money managers will claim there are just two types of stock market investment: Growth and Value. Growth seeks to find companies the investor believes have a long-term future. These are buy-and-hold investments. Value looks to buy under-priced stocks, based on any number of metrics, and to see them rise to a higher price.

There are as many ways to pick individual stocks as there are people. Everyone knows of a unique combination of fundamental (information about underlying business and economic realities) and technical (an analysis that focuses on market price and volume data) analysis for picking stocks. If the stock trader persists he or she will have a well-defined means of scanning for stocks, a set of entry signals defining when to take a position (long or short), entry order rules (limit, market, scale-in, double-down, etc.), and stop-loss, profit-target, and trailing stop rules. These are all part of serious trading. They are a large part of the e-mini day-trading system described in this book.

When trading individual stocks I encountered a number of hurdles which were difficult to overcome:

- Scanning for stocks, even with software automation, can be tedious, especially if one is reviewing results of stock scans on a regular basis.
- Unless a small basket of stocks are repeatedly traded, which defeats much of the purpose of stock scans, one doesn't learn the behavior of an individual stock. Not knowing a stock that's being traded leaves the practitioner with a sense of shooting at random, or gambling, especially when there are losses. (I am aware of serious stock traders who become knowledgeable with a number of individual stocks, which then becomes their universe of traded stocks. I never got to that point.)

- Even after carefully selecting a stock to buy or sell, if the trader's position is not aligned with the overall movement in the broader market (bull, bear), no stock picking system can be profitable.

It was this last point, and the idea that effective stock picking is probably best left to teams of analysts with techniques developed over many years, which turned me away from individual stock trading. Because no matter what Herculean efforts are thrown at stock scans and the selection process, if trading on the wrong side of the market, money is lost. So if I was going to have to get the broader market right in order to be a trader, I might as well just focus on that. And there are certainly enough ways today to trade the overall stock market.

After never doing that well trading stocks, and enamored with the greater aura of stock options, I went about looking for stock option systems to trade. This was the path I took when first leaving my job at Intel.

Stock Options

Trading stock options is more complicated than trading stocks and there is a huge amount of hype, education and promotion around the trading of stock options. Today, I can only smile when seeing an advertisement for a free, beginner's introduction to stock option trading at a local hotel ballroom. I've been to these, and am a little afraid for the Ma-and-Pa types in the room who may get snared. There are some incredible salespeople pitching options as a means to Easy Street. (Forex is similarly hyped today, maybe more so.) Despite all this, I was determined to trade stock options, holding on to the belief that an engineering background would give me an edge.

There are two basic types of options: Calls and Puts. A Call option gives the owner the right to purchase a stock at a fixed price some time in the future. A Put option gives the owner the right to sell a stock at a fixed price some time in the future.

Purchase a Call if you think a stock will increase in price. For example, if you think INTC (Intel) will rise from its current price of around $12 (February 2009), purchase a July $12 INTC Call (July is the expiration date of the contract; $12 is called the "Strike Price" of the contract). Now if INTC does in fact move above $12 you have the right to purchase INTC at $12 through July (the third Friday in July) and then sell it back at something more than $12 for a profit.

Currently, some four months before the July expiration, the $12 June Call can be purchased for about $1.50. Each contract "controls" 100 shares of INTC. If you purchased 10 $12 July INTC Calls you would make a 10 x 100 x $1.50 = $1500.00 investment. If INTC went to $15 at the time of expiration, your $12 Calls would be $3 "In-the-Money" (ITM) – meaning you can buy INTC for $12 with the rights from your Call contracts and turn around and sell the shares back to the market at the going price of $15 – a $3 profit. In total, your 10 Calls would be worth 10 x 100 x ($15 - $12) = 1000 x $3 = $3000. From an original outlay of $1500 you have gained $3000 - $1500 = $1500, a 100% return!

It's easy to become enamored with the idea of trading options. Of course if INTC doesn't get above $12 by July, you've lost the cost of your Call contract purchase, or $1500. A speculator who's willing to gamble that INTC won't get above $12 will gladly sell the Call options and pocket a $1500 premium for doing so.

Purchase a Put if you think a stock will decrease in price. If you think INTC is going to $10, purchase a $12 Put. If INTC is at $10 when the option contract expires, you will be $2 ITM and you can sell (short) INTC at $12 exercising your rights as the owner of Put contracts and then buy (cover) INTC back for $10. Again, speculators betting INTC will stay above $12 will be happy to sell $12 Put options.

As you can imagine, buyers and sellers of options trade contracts continuously and across a range of expiration dates and strike prices. The accurate pricing of options – why the $12 July INTC Call was worth $1.50 in February – is based on the underlying stock price, the specified strike price, the expiration date, the going interest rate (what you'd receive for your money if you were not in the market), and the perceived volatility in the market (the fear premium of the option contract quantifying the risk associated with trading a contract on an underlying stock that can quickly change in price). The pricing model was developed by financial mathematicians some 35 years ago and is referred to as the Black-Scholes formula. Its authors won the 1997 Nobel Prize in Economics. The Black-Scholes formula has created a gigantic financial industry for options on stocks, stock indices, futures, and other financial products.

Options, because they are a derivative (a contract derived from an underlying stock), can be used to create highly leveraged positions. In particular, the selling of options is fraught with dangerous obligations the seller may have to honor – say having to sell INTC shares at $12 when they are trading at $15. But there are sane ways to use options.

For example, if one is bullish on a stock, then purchasing a deep ITM Call with some reasonable expiration period can work. This is a way to invest in a stock you think is on the rise with much less capital than is required to buy shares of the stock outright.

Let's say one is bullish on Google (GOOG), an extraordinary company. Purchasing the shares outright at today's price of $350 is prohibitive for many small investors. On the other hand, one can currently buy a June 2009 $290 Call for the equivalent of $60 a share. This option currently has what is called a Delta[1] of 70, meaning the price of the option will move at approximately 70% the rate of the underlying GOOG shares.

If GOOG moves from $350 to $400, or $50, in the next couple of months, the Call option has a good chance of increasing in value from $60 to $60 + 0.70 x $50 = $95. The option will have appreciated $(95-60)/$60 = 58% over the course of the one to two months of GOOG price rise. On the other hand, if I had purchased GOOG outright at its current price of $350, it would have to increase to approximately $550 to realize an equivalent appreciation.

My $60 GOOG option will expire in June 2009, five months from now, and with its expiration, my $60 will be lost. If I purchase GOOG shares outright, I'll continue to own something of significant value, even if the stock does not appreciate. But one can see the allure of options: Get the complicated timing and contract specifications right and you can realize amazing returns.

Another example of how stock options can be profitably used comes from some of the folk-lore around the world-famous investor Warren Buffett.

---

[1] The Option Greeks: Delta, Gamma, Theta, Vega and Rho, are outputs of the Black-Scholes formula. Delta is the rate-of-change in option price with respect to the underlying stock price (a first derivative with respect to stock price). Gamma is the rate-of-change of Delta with stock price (a second derivative with respect to stock price). Theta is the rate-of-change in option price with respect to time (how fast the option loses value as we get closer to expiration; a first derivative with respect to time). Vega is a measure of option volatility (a quantification of how much uncertainty there is that the underlying stock will change). Rho is a measure of option price sensitivity to interest rate.

As the story goes, Buffett will determine a price at which he'd like to own a stock. Let's take Intel again as an example. Intel, even though a key global high-tech and industrial company with tremendous assets, is currently badly beaten down and trading for around $13, well below a price of $25 just six months ago.

Let's say Buffett has decided that $12 is an attractive price at which to buy INTC. Today he can Sell July 2009 $12 Put options for $1.25. Buffet's company will receive a premium of $1.25 per share as a result of selling the Puts. Importantly, the company will have also taken on the obligation of being "put" shares of INTC (thus the name, Put option), that is, required to purchase INTC at $12 per share, should the stock fall to that price between now and July 2009. But that is what he wanted to do anyway – own INTC. By selling the Put options for $1.25, Buffett has in effect realized a $1.25/$12.00 or 10% return the day he buys the shares. If INTC never falls to $12, Buffett's company will pocket the $1.25 per share income from the Put sale. Either way, not bad.

Remember, Buffett has the wherewithal to make good on the purchase of the $12 INTC shares, should INTC fall to that price. Selling options obligates the selling party to buy or sell stock at prices he or she would normally find undesirable, and which will often turn into a losing trade. Selling options is very dangerous.

There is much hype in the media that selling options can be an attractive means of generating income. Pick the right Calls and Puts to sell and pocket the seller's premium, while protecting oneself from an event where the stock price falls below (Puts) or rises above (Calls) the options strike price. Finding a means of such protection is the hard part. But if one is an engineer or mathematician at heart, finding a means of hedging your bets in a calculated fashion is an inviting challenge. At least that was my thinking.

In the Spring of 2003 I began selling what are known as Covered Put and Call Spreads, below and above support and resistance price levels, on individual stocks. These spreads are also called "Covered Short Strangles," for those more familiar with options trading. This is a widely known and publicized means of generating income. An option spread is created by selling an option with a strike price relatively close to the market and purchasing an offsetting, hedging option further from the market. The purchased options, one's hedge, is where the phrase "covered" originates.

In short, the covered spread trader is selling an insurance policy at a strike price relatively close to the market. To protect this position, he is purchasing his own insurance at a less risky level in the market. The difference between insurance sold and insurance bought is the collected premium. An example helps.

It's Spring 2003 and eBay (EBAY), the famous online auctioneer, has been on a relentless rally, now trading at close to $90 and with what looks like good support at the $75 level.

I sold 30 April 2003 70x65 Put spreads: 30 April 2003 $70 Puts are sold and 30 April 2003 $65 Puts are bought. The transaction netted $1538 in premium collected. That amount is the difference in the price of the options sold and those bought.

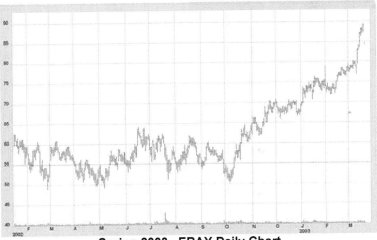

Spring 2003. EBAY Daily Chart

If EBAY falls precipitously, I am protected by owning the $65 Put. In this case, my worst case loss, no matter what, is ($70 - $65) x 100 x 30 minus the premium collected, or $15000 - $1538 = $13462. If EBAY begins to slowly break-down and heads for the inner $70 Put that I've sold, I can buy back the spread for a little more than what I sold it for. That's a mental stop-loss that needs to be monitored daily and executed or not, depending on how the market behaves and how much the EBAY Put spread increases in value from where I originally sold it. The next chart shows the EBAY Put spread.

Ideally, April 2003 expiration (the third Friday in April) will arrive and EBAY will still be above the $70 inner strike price, the options will expire worthless and I will keep the full $1538 premium. That is what happened with this trade. By executing these types of spreads below (Puts) and above (Calls) the market, with a number of different stocks and contract sizes, I sought to generate a regular monthly income.

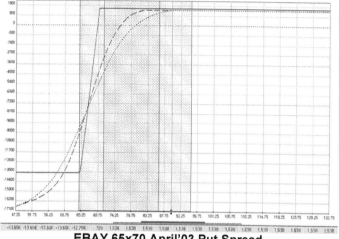

EBAY 65x70 April'03 Put Spread

This all works well until market volatility increases too much. Stock option prices fluctuate wildly when there is increased uncertainty. Covered spread selling works best when there is moderate volatility in the market. If there is too little volatility, option prices are low, maybe too low to make selling option spreads worthwhile, and the seller may be lured into selling dangerously close to the market to increase his premium. But if volatility is too high, then options prices can fluctuate so much that the trader has his hand forced quickly – options must be re-purchased at a significant loss – because who can know how far up or down the market will go? The options trader doesn't need to be caught too many times with his or her spread going in-the-money (the stock price reaches the inner leg of the options spread – $70 in the EBAY example) to realize it's better to be safe than sorry when it comes to selling options.

There are numerous tools and techniques that have been developed to manage the kind of spread trading touched on here. This includes a variety of techniques to hedge options with the underlying stock (long or short) and with other options, in the same or different month of expiration. It is a huge and fascinating game that has attracted the best financial and trading minds.

When I was trading stock options in this manner, I would do quite well for several months in a row, but then have a mini blow-up. The market would move quickly against a position and I would have to close it for a significant loss, sometimes four or five times more than the premium collected. These mini blow-ups would wipe out months of profitable income. The practice of writing options is much more difficult than the retail trade press lets on.

There were three important take-aways from my experience with stock options spread trading, which led to a next stage of options trading.

1. Trading stock options is the same as trading the underlying stock in one important respect: For all the care and sophistication one might bring to trading options, the single biggest determinant of success remains making a correct decision on the price of the underlying stock and the market as a whole. Options do not, with their new, sophisticated models, remove the trader from the task of getting the market right, in fact they make it even more important to read the market correctly.
2. While proponents of selling options for income repeatedly point to the fact that greater than 90% of all options expire worthless, so that it makes sense to collect a premium on something that will quickly become worthless, what they fail to mention is how bad it can be if caught on the wrong side of the other 10% that don't expire, and which finish in-the-money or must be re-purchased at a cost far exceeding the original premium collected.
3. Individual stocks, because of earnings announcements, analyst upgrades and downgrades, or other conditions, can take dramatic price swings – overnight gaps – and these swings make the selling of individual stock options difficult.

It is because of this last point that the next step in options premium collection evolution is to move from individual stock to stock index options.

Stock Index Options

The Chicago Board Options Exchange (CBOE) is the largest stock option exchange in the world. It was spun off from the Chicago Board of Trade (CBOT) in 1973 to standardize the trading of stock options. On its first day, 911 options contracts were traded on 16 stocks. At this writing, a typical day will see over three million contracts traded on thousands of stocks, market indexes, and other derivative products.

CBOE market data currently shows approximately 10 million open contracts on the S&P 500 Index[2]. These options are referenced with the symbol SPX. There are almost another 10 million contracts open on the S&P 500 SPY ETF (Exchange Traded Fund). Today there is an enormous market of options contracts that can be traded on the S&P 500 and related indices. For the spread trading program just described these options can be used to eliminate price volatility inherent in a single stock.

In the case of stock options, or ETF options for that matter, option pricing is directly tied to the underlying stock price and based on the 100 shares per option contract specification. For example, if GOOG is at $300 when a GOOG $290 Call option expires, the option will be worth $10 x 100 or $1000. That is because the GOOG $290 Call gives the owner the right to buy 100 shares of GOOG for $290, which he or she can then turn around and sell for $300. When based on a stock index, it's not exactly clear how to price an option.

What the CBOE has done is turn the index into a cash price by assigning a value of $100 to each point in the index. Now the index value looks like a stock price when figuring the value of an index option. Let's say I purchase an SPXBCT, the March 2009 900 SPX Call (every option contract is given a unique alphabetic code beginning with its underlying symbol, SPX in the case of the S&P 500 Index). The SPXBCT contract is currently trading for approximately $20. If the S&P 500 index reaches 910 on or before the third Friday in March, 2009, my SPXBCT will be in-the-money. At expiration, assuming the index is at exactly 910, the CBOE will settle my position in cash. For every contract I will be credited

---

[2] The S&P 500 (Standard & Poor's 500) is a collection of 500 of the most highly capitalized (number of outstanding shares x stock price) companies selected from across the major sectors of the U.S. economy. The S&P 500 Index is constructed as a weighted average based on capitalization. It is a broad measure of the overall stock market and considered a leading indicator of U.S. economic activity.

(910 - 900) x $100 = $1000. So SPX makes the underlying stock index look like a stock, while giving the trader the benefit of trading a broad market index. This $100 per index point value will become crucial when comparing stock index options with stock index futures options, which we will do later.

When trading a broad index, like the S&P 500, one uses statistical standard deviation and similar measures of price dispersion to make trading decisions, and the sudden gaps that can occur in a single stock price are eliminated. That is not to say that there haven't been extreme moves in the stock market (just look at Sept-Oct 2008 to see this!), but in general, it is easier to deal with the movement of the S&P 500 than any single stock.

The type of trade described with EBAY now became my focus using stock index options. On January 30, 2009, with the S&P 500 Index near 850, a possible position might be:

- Sell 10 SPX 700 Feb09 Put @ $5.00; Buy 10 SPX 660 Feb09 Put @ $1.75. Collect 10 x $100 x (5.00 – 1.75) = $3250.
- Sell 10 SPX 920 Feb09 Call @ 4.00; Buy 10 SPX 960 Feb09 Call @ 1.00. Collect 10 x $100 x (4.00 – 1.00) = $3000.

Together this generates an income of $6250 for February. Now all we have to do is hope the market doesn't approach our inner strike prices of 700 and 920 over the next three weeks. We will monitor the market, using support and resistance levels, historical volatility and standard deviation calculations, changes in the option Greek values, and other tools. If the market gets too close to our inner strike prices, we will have to close the position, perhaps opening new, differently placed spreads to offset some of the loss from the buy-back. More sophisticated traders will take long and short positions in the underlying, for example using the SPY ETF. The most sophisticated traders will sell the options naked – no purchased outer-leg options to hedge the options sold. This requires more nerve and more account margin.

As for the account margin required to hold the example here, the exchange will typically calculate a value based on the full spread value, and require 100% of that amount, minus the premium collected. For example, the full value of the Put and Call spreads is 10 x $100 x 40 = $40,000, because the spreads are 40 index points wide (700 – 660; 960 – 920). But importantly the exchange will typically only require half of the full value of the Put plus Call position, because it can be assumed that the market will move in one direction or the other, but not both like a whipsaw, over the expiration of the contracts. And the exchange will incorporate the option premium collected in the margin calculation.

Given these assumptions, margin will only be required for one side of the combined Put and Call positions and something less than the value of the full spread width. So, if we are lucky to have all contracts expire worthless, we will realize a $6250/($40,000-$6250) = 18% ROI in about three weeks. And you can see why this type of trading is so compelling!

On a more mundane level, large investors will use SPX options not to speculate, the way the options spread trader speculates month-to-month, but as a hedge. A large collection of individual stocks can be protected with a hedge made up of purchased SPX Puts. If the portfolio of stocks moves down too much, it is almost assured that the S&P 500 Index has too, in which case the SPX Puts increase in value and offset the stock losses.

But purchasing Puts can be expensive, so how does the hedge fund pay for them? One method is with the sale of Call options above the market. This "collars" the fund's portfolio. If just the right balance of stocks owned, index Puts bought and index Calls sold is maintained, a fund can protect its investments and still offer a modest return, say 7%, using the collaring technique.

Incidentally, Bernard Madoff, notorious for having been caught running a $50B(!) Ponzi scheme, Wall Street's worst investment scam ever, claimed to use the collaring technique as the basis for his fund's profits. Experienced professionals know that getting more than approximately 7% from the technique on a regular basis is pretty much impossible. Madoff's 10-15% returns, year after year, were one of the obvious inconsistencies that tipped off those knowledgeable with options. When Madoff was confronted with this discrepancy he attempted to deflect criticism by saying something to the effect that other funds were not implementing the system correctly – a vague and disingenuous response as we now know.

Futures

I first came into contact with commodity futures from references in popular culture to pork bellies and orange juice. The movie comedy Trading Places (1983) with Dan Aykroyd and Eddie Murphy was loosely based on a well-known experiment and wager between commodity traders Richard Dennis and William Eckhardt over the nature-nurture question in educating new traders (see the Trade Examples chapter). I'd heard something of Hillary Clinton's dubious trades with cattle futures in the late 1970s. When I read Market Wizards, by Jack Schwager, there were numerous references to futures traders.

Looking for an edge in my stock scanning, I naively believed there might be one for me trading commodity futures, where the underlying asset often has some seasonal predictability that can be exploited. I read Investing in Wheat, Soybeans, Corn, by the famous grain trader William Grandmill, and tried to learn and trade his methods. But with a stock and stock option background I naturally gravitated to equity index futures – futures contracts based on popular stock indices.

Typically, futures contracts have been bought and sold to hedge and speculate on the production and consumption of commodities: Agricultural products (corn, soybeans, wheat, cattle, pork bellies, orange juice); Precious metals (gold, silver, platinum); Energies (crude oil, natural gas); and Softs (cocoa, cotton, coffee). Commodities futures traders are known for their quick and large profits and losses, and trading commodity futures has the reputation of being the last, and most serious, market in which to trade, based on the minimal margin requirements and purported sharp swings in commodity prices. In fact, academic studies have found that commodity futures prices show no greater volatility than stocks.

The S&P 500 index futures were first offered on the floor of the Chicago Mercantile Exchange (CME, or "The Merc") in 1982. They were jokingly referred to as "pin-stripe" futures because of their stock index and cash settlement basis. The issue the inventors of the S&P 500 index futures had to grapple with, in order to make them a reality, was, How will settlement work for a futures contract that is based on a stock market index? Can we settle the contract to a basket of stocks that is the equivalent of the S&P 500 Index?

Commodity futures of the past settled in quantities of the underlying commodity. If I buy a September 2009 soybean futures contract at $8.00, then I have the right to purchase 5000 bushels of soybeans shortly after the September 2009 contract expires. With a long position from $8.00 I am guaranteed the right to purchase the soybeans at $8.00 a bushel. Buying a soybean futures contract is similar to purchasing a Call option on a stock, where owning the Call gives me the right to purchase the stock at the strike price of the option. A soybean speculator might purchase a September 2009 soybeans futures contract at $8.00 if he or she thought the price of soybeans would rise above $8.00 a bushel by September.

If I am a producer of soybeans, say a soybean farmer, then I have some fixed production costs that must be recovered with my harvest. I want to lock in a floor price at which I can sell my soybeans. In this case, I will short a soybeans futures contract. If I short the September 2009 contract from $8.00, then I am guaranteed the right to sell 5000 bushels of soybeans at $8.00 a bushel shortly after the September 2009 contract expires.

If I am a consumer of soybeans, say a manufacturer of soy sauce, then I might purchase futures contracts in order to set a ceiling on how much I will have to pay for the soybeans I need to manufacture soy sauce. Again, a long position from $8.00 in the September 2009 soybean futures contract gives me the right to purchase soybeans in September at $8.00 a bushel.

The way in which the exchange matches buyers and sellers, hedgers and speculators, without any direct contact between trading parties, is one of the amazing features of the open market and exchange system. Another key benefit of futures is the way the exchange sets precise specifications for what is being traded and actually delivered. Futures contracts standardize commodity markets.

So how should settlement work for a futures contract based on the S&P 500 Index? At first glance, one would expect to deliver, or take ownership of, a collection of stocks, in varying amounts, representing the components of the S&P 500 Index. But is that feasible for an index consisting of 500 companies and with the goal of supporting, potentially, millions of futures contracts changing hands?

As in the case of the CBOE index option, the inventors of the S&P 500 index futures, now referred to as SPs, decided on a purely cash settlement basis. Every SP point is valued at $250 (originally it was $500), and this becomes the basis for settlement pricing. An example works best.

Let's say I am long the March 2009 SP futures contract from 850.00. (The "tick," or smallest increment of change, in the SP contract, is 0.10 points, and so worth $25.00.) If the S&P 500 Index opens on the third Friday of March, 2009, at 860.00, which is exactly when all the March 2009 SP contracts expire, then the cash settlement of my contract will be a credit of (860.00 – 850.00) x $250 = $2500.00 in my futures trading account. If I were short the same contract from 850.00, then my account would be debited by an equal amount. Everything settles to cash, which is preferred to an underlying stock settlement that, while matching traditional commodity futures settlement, is impractical.

As you might expect, no one actually waits for settlement to occur. Rather, SP contracts are actively traded and closed prior to expiration, and it is the constant trading of SP contracts which provides the liquidity for those participants using SP futures to hedge a stock portfolio.

SP contracts are issued quarterly, with March, June, September and December expirations. Contracts expire at the open of the day session on the third Friday of the quarterly expiration month. Active trading moves to the next quarter's contract at the open of the Thursday overnight session, one week before the Friday expiration, so that active traders do not have to be concerned with expiration issues.

SP futures originally traded in an open outcry pit at the CME. As the commodity exchanges moved to electronically traded contracts, the pit and the electronic contracts traded side-by-side in a hybrid trading environment, which continues today. A fascinating aspect of the hybrid system is the way the pit and electronic contracts stay within a few ticks of one another. Sophisticated traders may simultaneously trade both contracts, looking for arbitrage scalping opportunities between the two.

The E-Mini

In 1997 the CME introduced the S&P 500 index futures "e-mini" contract (electronically traded, mini-sized). Referred to as the ES (Electronic SP), it has one-fifth the value of the larger SP, so that one ES point is equivalent to $50. Because of its smaller valuation, the ES tick is relatively larger than the SP's, taking increments of quarter points, .00, .25, .50 and .75, with one tick worth $50/4 or $12.50.

The ES contract attracts tens of thousands of traders around the world, and almost 24 hours a day. (There are brief periods during the week when the electronic platform, called Globex, is taken off-line for maintenance. There is a 48 hour period on the weekend – Friday afternoon to Sunday afternoon – when the Globex does not trade.) With the ubiquity of high-speed internet access, low commissions, excellent liquidity, and the margin and tax advantages of trading futures (more about this later), retail traders have shown particular fondness for the ES contract.

The ES contract today trades in volumes that far exceed the original SP contract. Recent monthly volume figures for the ES and SP contracts are shown in the table below. (Note that the larger December volumes are due primarily to December being a contract expiration month.)

SP open outcry persists for historical reasons and some local traders continue to earn a living at it. Institutional clients may achieve a small edge in commissions with the SP contract or prefer to have their large orders completed with the full bid-ask control of a human trader. And the pit does provide some information which the electronic trader, seated half-a-world away, does not get – the knowledge of a large order about to be placed and the roar, up and down, in the pit.

	Dec-08	Jan-09
SP (Open Outcry and Globex)	1,167, 283	674,413
ES	55,256,862	45,814,102
NQ	11,604,398	5,713,178
YM	4,414,444	3,707,910
TF (ICE/NYBOT)	4,091,416	2,475,277

Equity Index Futures Monthly Trading Volumes

Today there are streaming audio internet services which the ES trader can use to realize actual pit noise and activity. However, open outcry is fast becoming an anachronism and its days are numbered. The ES contract has become the favorite futures contract of both large and small traders.

In addition to the ES contract, three other e-mini futures contracts are popular and traders who make use of the ES will often use these and look for price irregularities, or divergences, among the four against which to trade. The CME NQ contract is an e-mini contract based on the Nasdaq 100 Index. One NQ point is worth $20 and its ticks are quarter points, similar to the ES contract, and worth $5. The CME YM e-mini contract (originally from the Chicago Board of Trade or CBOT) is a DJIA based contract, whose tick is the same as one point and worth $5. The ICE TF contract (previously a CME contract now owned by the Intercontinental Exchange/New York Board of Trade, ICE/NYBOT) is based on the small-cap stock Russell 2000 Index. Its contract point is worth $100 and has ticks in increments of 0.10 point worth $10.

From the above volume figures, it's easy to see that the ES contract is by far the most popular, trading at five to ten times the volume of the next most popular NQ contract, and roughly 10 times that of the YM and TF. Because the Nasdaq 100 and DJIA indices have fewer components (100 and 30), NQ and YM futures prices can be readily compared with their underlying index, referred to as the "cash" market, and some traders make use of this.

Conveniently, the four contracts have been designed so that tick prices are, for the most part, normalized. For example, the DJIA moves numerically at approximately 10 times that of the S&P 500 Index. 20 YM points should correspond to two ES points and, in fact, 20 YM points are worth $100 as are two ES points. This makes it easier for the trader to move between the equity index futures. However, each has its own unique performance subtleties.

There are both intra-day (no contracts held over night) and over-night margin requirements for the e-mini futures contracts. Intra-day margins can be as little as $500 per contract. Overnight margins are typically $2500-$4000. Depending on the trader's relationship with his broker and the exchange, margin requirements can vary. The exchange has the right to modify margin requirements when market volatility or other factors change.

Introducing Brokers, or IBs, through which the retail trader will deal for access to the exchange, provide a single commission schedule for an e-mini trade (which includes fees for the IB, the FCM, or Futures Commission Merchant, a member of the Exchange, and the Exchange itself). These are roughly $3 to $5 per contract for a "round-turn," which includes opening (buy or sell) and closing (sell or buy) a contract. Volume and exchange member discounts at various levels are also available.

Trading futures (and futures options, see below) has distinct tax advantages. Intra-day trading profits in these instruments are taxed as capital gains with a 60/40 long-term/short-term capital gain ratio. Short-term profits from trading stocks and stock options are generally taxed as ordinary income.

Much more will be said about trading the ES, NQ, YM and TF contracts, individually and as a "4-plex" of inter-related markets. Although this introduction covers a number of market descriptions, the focus of the book is trading these four e-minis.

Options on Futures

Just as with stocks, one can buy or sell Calls and Puts on a futures contract. Futures options can be used by the hedger to purchase the rights to a long or short futures position, at a predetermined price, and without the exposure to daily "marked-to-market" requirements inherent with holding an actual futures position.

Marked-to-market is a reckoning of account value based on a trader's opening contract price and the daily settlement price of the futures contracts in which the trader has "open interest" – an existing long or short position. If the market moves significantly against a trader's position, there can be an account margin call, with deposit due before the beginning of the next trading session. If the margin call goes unmet, the trader's account may be automatically closed. Options remove the user from marked-to-market exposure.

Returning to the soybean futures example, if the consumer of soybeans desires to lock in a ceiling price paid for the commodity, a Call can be purchased on a soybean futures contract. A Call strike price that is at the desired ceiling price and in-the-money will settle to an assigned long futures position from that price, giving its owner the right to purchase the commodity at the ceiling price. If the producer of soybeans desires to lock in a floor price paid for the commodity, a Put can be purchased on a soybean futures contract. A Put strike price that is at the desired floor price and in-the-money will settle to an assigned short futures position from that price, giving its owner the right to sell the commodity at the floor price. Hedgers will buy Calls and Puts; speculators will buy and sell them; and the exchange will provide a means of matching hedgers and speculators without any direct contact between the two.

Futures options are based on underlying futures contracts with quarterly expirations, March, June, September and December in the case of SP and ES futures. The options contracts themselves are issued with expirations on any month. For example, I might purchase a February 900.00 SP Call, which is a Call option expiring in February on the March SP futures contract with a strike price of 900. Options which expire with the underlying quarterly futures contract (e.g., March, June, September, December) are referred to as quarterly options. Options which expire off the quarterly cycle, as in the case of the February Call example, are referred to as serial options. There are subtle differences in expiration timing for quarterly and serial options, which the reader can ignore, unless he or she is interested in actively trading futures options.

Today there are options on both the SP and ES contracts. As with the futures, ES options, the electronic equivalent of the original SP option, control one-fifth the value of SP options. SP options are traded through open outcry – there is a small pit just off the main SP futures pit on the floor of the CME. Traders need to have access to a Futures Commission Merchant (FCM) agent on the floor, via phone, SMS text, Internet, or equivalent, in order to place orders, or alternatively work with their broker who will place orders on their behalf.

While ES options are entirely electronic, SP options continue to retain some advantages for the trader (the commission schedule to contract size, open outcry bid-ask negotiation), but ES options, like the underlying ES futures contract before it, are quickly gaining ground on open outcry trading, and an attractive market of electronically traded ES options is developing along-side the ES futures.

Recent monthly volume figures for the ES and SP option contracts are shown in the table below. Note that for December, 2008, the SP options continued to be roughly three-and-a-half times as large as the ES options, when underlying futures contract size is considered ((1.48 x 5) / 2.12 = 3.5).

	Dec-08	Jan-09
SP (Open Outcry)	1,482,529	1,003,412
ES	2,119,296	1,285,498

Equity Index Futures Options Monthly Trading Volumes

With both CBOE SPX options and CME SP options the stock index options trader has two contracts to choose from. Futures options enjoy the capital gain tax treatment described earlier. In addition, CME futures margin calculation uses the SPAN (Standard Portfolio ANalysis) system, a methodology that purportedly analyzes the "what-ifs" of market conditions and more aggressively sets futures margin requirements. The bottom-line is that futures margin requirements are less stringent than the fixed point calculations used with stock. As a rule of thumb with futures options spreads, one can multiply the spread width by 50% as part of the margin calculation. This is shown in the following table, where the futures option is almost twice as efficient as the index option for similar 20-point covered spreads.

This type of calculation led me to begin trading, in 2005, SP futures options spreads, using the same short strangle strategy as described earlier with SPX index options. But just as in the case of using index options, while my trading could proceed for many months profitably, it would incur a mini-blow up when the market became volatile.

Option	$/pt	Commiss Per Contract	No. Contracts	Commiss	Spread Width	Premium Pts
SP (CME)	250.00	15.00	10	300	20	1.0
SPX (CBOE)	100.00	1.50	10	30	20	1.0

Option	Premium	Maint. Margin Factor	Maint. Margin Calculated	Net	ROI %
SP (CME)	2500.00	0.50	22500.00	2200.00	9.8
SPX (CBOE)	1000.00	1.00	19000.00	970.00	5.1

Futures Options vs. Index Options Margin Comparison

While I enjoyed calling down to the floor of the CME and working with the pit agents to complete my orders, I stopped selling options just after the February 27, 2007 sell-off when the Dow dropped more than 400 points in a single day, and which eventually resulted in wiping out six months of trading profits in my account.

When stock market volatility greatly increased in 2008 many experienced and professionally run SP option selling programs lost significantly more than 50% of their account value and were closed. I was lucky to get out when I did.

TradeStation and Mechanical Systems

It is true that for all the care and sophistication one might bring to trading options, the single biggest determinant of success remains making a correct decision on the price of the underlying asset and the market as a whole. When I took an advanced options trading course at the CBOE, once the instructor had covered the mechanics of options, specific positions would be used to illustrate options trading and the examples undoubtedly began with a technical analysis. Specific technical indicators were referenced and students were encouraged to bring additional indicators to their position analysis. I realized it was important to find a good PC platform for running technical analysis.
After reviewing a number of systems I settled on the TradeStation desktop.

I continue to be impressed with TradeStation, now some five years after first beginning to use it. For charting and signal generation, using canned, pre-existing indicators or developing new ones, I think it's unmatched in the retail trading industry. Most of the charts in this book were produced using TradeStation.

TradeStation is much more than charts and indicators. A strong focus of the product is automated strategy development, testing and online execution. The TradeStation desktop, which includes a very accessible and full-featured programming language, called EasyLanguage, is an excellent platform for fast prototyping trade strategies and quickly determining their validity with back-testing on historical data. For the most sophisticated user, TradeStation can automatically execute trades from EasyLanguage programs developed by the programmer-trader. To this end, the desktop includes a middleware layer, referred to as TradeManager, for assisting in automating all aspects of mechanical system order execution. And there is a mature community of online forums, consultants and third-party software that make up the TradeStation ecosystem.

TradeStation marketing espouses the idea of trade strategy automation, or mechanical systems trading, as a means of removing the emotion from trading. The message is to spend time upfront building and testing mechanical systems and then let the computer make money for you. Discretionary trading, with all its human emotion, is replaced with trading that is well-defined and determined solely from technical indicator calculation. It sounds compelling at first, especially if one is a computer programmer interested in trading.

Institutional investment firms and hedge funds have long since embraced mechanical systems. Jim Simons, the well-known mathematician and founder of the extraordinarily successful Renaissance Technologies investment company, is quoted as saying all his trading decisions are 100% automated. A review of financial employment websites (e.g., eFinancialCareers.com) shows strong demand for programmer-traders with "high-frequency" trading experience; i.e., computer-based, mechanical trading. TradeStation offers the individual retail trader the opportunity to mechanize as well.

Once having become experienced with TradeStation EasyLanguage and some of the basics of strategy back-testing, I would scour trade magazines and books looking for strategies to code and test. For example, I programmed and tested many of the strategies described in Trade Like a Hedge Fund, by James Altucher.

I tested Altucher's Unilateral Pairs Trading on a variety of asset pairs and could generate impressive five year equity curves, like the NQ-DIA example (DJIA ETF; one NQ contract traded) shown in the next graph.

I was well aware of curve-fitting and how one could be fooled with a trading Holy Grail result from back-testing. So I made sure to keep input parameters to a minimum, and whenever there were parameters that could be tuned to historical data, I would make sure they were assigned sensible values and then fix them. For example, I might set a stop-loss level at 2% of contract value, a fairly reasonable value regardless of the strategy tested.

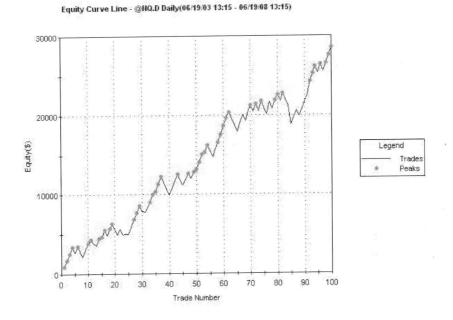

Equity Curve Line - @NQ.D Daily(06/19/03 13:15 - 06/19/08 13:15)

NQ-DIA Uni-Pairs Equity Curve (6/03-6/08)

But even given a conservative approach, look at the next chart and see how the exact same strategy performed up to this writing (February 2009). How many could stomach a 40% draw-down, knowing it is generated purely by software?

I executed this system and others like it on actual trading accounts using TradeStation automation to handle all aspects of trading. I found mechanical systems do not eliminate the emotions of trading. While removing one from individual trade decisions, it is maddening to see computer programs lose money as you stand to the side.

I developed an intra-day scalping program for the ES contract that showed promise in back-testing. Based on a well-known mean-reverting algorithm it produced an extraordinary equity curve; see the following graph (Scalper Holy Grail, three year back-test; one ES contract traded). Had I found the Holy Grail?

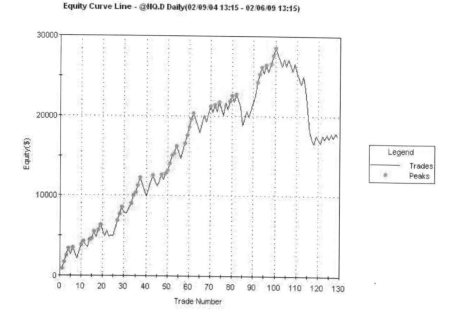

NQ-DIA Uni-Pairs Equity Curve (2/04-2/09)

When I ran the program against the market, actual limit order fill rates were less than theoretical back-test results. As a scalping program, the system was sensitive to small changes in live performance and this version of the trading Holy Grail did not make money (but it didn't lose either!). Actual account to strategy results for a recent two month period are shown in the chart below. The result was published in a Futures Magazine article, "Can Automated Scalping Work for Retail?", September, 2008, as a case study of strategy back-test to actual account performance for a fully automated strategy.

While I continue to research fully automated mechanical systems, my current e-mini day-trading takes a hybrid approach: Specific indicators and tools for helping make trade decisions, but ultimately all trade entry decisions are made on a discretionary basis. Once in a position, trade management is mostly automated; more about this later in the book.

I have found the hybrid approach to be the most satisfying. The e-mini stock index futures provide an outstanding opportunity to execute such a hybrid trading strategy. Again, trading is about finding a niche that works.

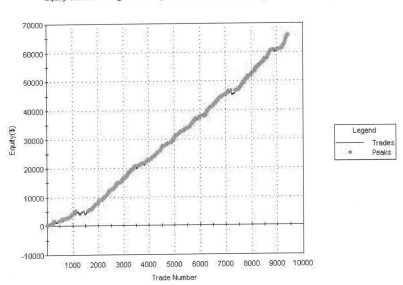

Scalper Holy Grail (2/05-2/08)

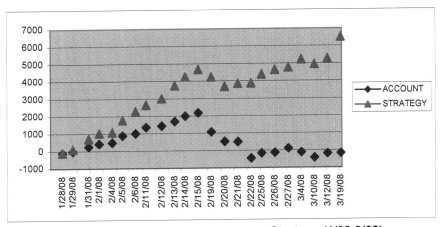

Scalper Live Trading Account vs. Strategy (1/08-3/08)

Day-Trading the E-Mini

E-mini stock index futures are an ideal market and day-trading them an ideal time-frame for a number of reasons:

Numerous stock market internals to assist the trader. Technical analysis of the stock index futures is rich and offers unique trading opportunities. From the stock markets (what the futures trader refers to as the cash market) come an abundance of data that can be used to assist the electronic futures trader. Index Price Levels; Up-Tick/Down-Tick counts; Advance/Decline ratios; Real-time Put/Call ratios; Volume. The futures exchanges offer additional information: Contract Volumes and Order Book Market Depth. All this data is available in real-time and can be analyzed in numerous combinations up to the skill-level of the trader.

Cross-market analysis. Because there are four popular e-mini stock index futures contracts (ES, NQ, YM, TF) price divergences among them can be exploited. This is similar to how, for example, gold and silver or oil and natural gas futures are traded in pairs. If the NQ is considered a leader and selling, while the YM contract is considered a follower and seen to be lagging, then shorting YM can potentially be a good trade.

No over-night positions. After writing options for several years and living with the possibility of an adverse over-night event, it is a pleasant relief to be flat at the end of every trading day. My account is entirely in cash as I sleep through the night. I feel in control trading this way. Margins are lower when there are no over-night positions open.

Low cost-of-entry. Assuming $5000-$10000 of account margin per e-mini contract traded, which is generous by most standards, and provides a cushion for surviving temporary draw-downs, a small capital investment is needed to begin trading one to four e-mini contracts. Trading at this size is adequate to learn sophisticated trading skills, earn some income, and advance to larger trading sizes when becoming more expert.

Excellent ROI possibilities for account growth or regular income. If day-trading the e-minis profitably, which means keeping losing days down to a 1-2% account debit, then it may be possible to realize a weekly 5% return on an account. Day-trading the e-minis has the possibility of growing an account or realizing a respectable income. That doesn't mean it's easy to day-trade, but there is a potential for someone who has the desire to learn.

Good market liquidity, low cost commissions and tax advantages. The e-mini stock index futures market has become very large, which translates into instantaneous fills and practically zero slippage when filling small orders. Round-turn e-mini commissions are $5 or less, even for the smallest retail account. Significantly lower commissions are available to volume traders. Profits are treated as capital gains, not regular income.

Sophisticated and reasonably priced desktop platforms to access the exchanges and execute trades. The latest generation of direct-access brokers gives the retail customer high-speed connectivity to the electronic exchanges. The platform and access subscription fees are modest and the latest generation of PCs provide sufficient horsepower to execute multiple desktop instances (multiple LCD displays) using a single subscription line. Sophisticated trading tools are now part of the retail trading desktop. As will be seen in the chapter that describes trade execution, the software to enter trades and automate trade execution has reached a level that supports high-frequency retail futures trading. This includes features such as exchange order book real-time simulation, so that the beginning trader can practice without jeopardizing an actual account. Readily available, low-cost internet broadband access, with low latencies, supports high-frequency retail trading.

Day-Trading Psychology

It is important to understand that day-trading, the e-minis or any market for that matter, requires sacrifice and discipline from the trader. To be completely forth-right, the prospective day-trader must honestly consider the following:

Day-trading means trading every day. Are you prepared to trade every day (or at least most days)? Personally, I enjoy taking on the market every day and the immediacy of it. I worked for more than 25 years in the computer industry, many of those as a manager, with all the meetings and team coordination that that entails. For me, the activity of trading, with immediate and concrete success or failure, is a joy. You must honestly enjoy the activity to be good at it. Leading trade psychologists make this point. Some days it can feel repetitious and at times meaningless, staring at screens for long periods of the day. I have great respect for anyone who attempts to become a day-trader. There is a bit of the heroic to it.

Day-trading means developing a specific skill. Are you prepared to invest the large amount of time and effort it will take to become profitable? Because you will not get there overnight. I have a strong urge to be competent at specific, well-defined tasks. I enjoyed learning to play the violin, with all the repetition of scales and études; I enjoyed tennis lessons and hitting practice balls repeatedly. I'd rather be a skilled practitioner of a specific discipline than a generalist. Day-traders, as a rule, are isolated specialists. It is probably the case that day-trading is not a skill that transfers directly to other professions (perhaps the closest match would be an air traffic controller).

Day-trading means repeated cycles of success and failure and recovering from failure, and living with the consequent emotions. Day-trading is, to a great extent, about playing a game of large numbers. Many losing trades will be inter-mixed with many winning trades. If practiced correctly, the percentage of winners times the average winning size minus the percentage of losers times the average losing size will be positive and one's account will steadily grow or income can be steadily made. The expected value of the endeavor will be positive, but the trader must endure a large number of losses. 2:1 winning odds is respectable in day-trading, which means a third of one's trades will be losers. I have had many moments of complete exasperation and frustration day-trading and been close to throwing in the towel. Day-trading has brought me to tears when I am otherwise quite stoic.

What does work is: (1) Finding a system that one can believe in because when it is executed correctly expected value is positive; (2) The system is simple enough to accurately execute repeatedly; and (3) One is committed to developing the self-discipline needed to stick to the trading system's rules.

If you are aware that the rules have been broken (and you will be when it happens!), then a discipline that stops trading for the day may be needed. Keeping a journal of winning and losing trades is a good idea. More will be said about the psychology of trading later in the text, and with specific examples and techniques to help the trader.

The next chapter covers enough trading basics so that a well-defined trading system can be explained in detail.

Trading Basics

The trading system described in this book is eclectic. As the reader will see, it takes ideas from a number of areas and combines them into a set of trading rules.

The system is best distinguished by the combination of technical analyses and indicators it uses. A guiding principle of the system is that there is no one technical indicator that is sufficient to trade profitably. It is from a combination of techniques that high probability trades are found.

Furthermore, indicators should not simply replicate each other. For example, experience with the technical indicators Stochastics and MACD (see below) show that they give roughly the same information. So that making use of both indicators does not improve the trader's view of the market, even as it might give a false sense of confidence; i.e., an additional tool has been put to use and as such will improve the trader's performance.

In reading about the various technical methods on which this trading system is built, one should see a range of approaches to collecting and organizing information about the market.

The trading system consists of specific trades derived from a number of technical analyses and perspectives:

- Market Profile Theory
- Market Internal Data
- Price Levels
- Price Extension and Retracement
- Price Patterns
- Time-of-Day Patterns
- Inter-Market Analysis
- Multi-Frame Charting

The text will document the way in which these various technical areas have been brought together into a single, coherent trading system. In order to fully understand the system and use it effectively, the trader needs to know some details of these techniques – he or she must look under the hood and not blindly trade a black box.

To that end, this chapter gives background information on each of the technical areas the e-mini stock index futures day-trading system uses to define its specific signals and setups. This chapter also covers important price action and order entry concepts needed to complete the Trading Basics background. (Note: The next chapter, Price Patterns, is devoted to price pattern analysis).

Finally, many professional traders advocate trading opening gaps – days when the stock index futures open gap up or gap down from the previous day's close – and this chapter covers some research analyzing opening gaps to determine if the setup will be part of the e-mini trading system advocated here.

The chapter provides the background necessary to make best use of the specific trade setups that will be detailed later in the book.

The Market Profile

The Market Profile was first described in 1984 by the well-known and highly-regarded commodity trader J. Peter Steidlmeyer. It was disseminated and popularized at the CBOT over the next 15 years.

An authoritative text on The Market Profile is Mind Over Markets, by James Dalton, Eric Jones and Robert Dalton. There has been a resurgence of interest in The Market Profile in the last several years, especially in the active electronic day-trading community.

There is significant substance to the Market Profile theory, but it is often unclear as to specifically how to trade it. For the purposes of day-trading the e-mini stock index futures, we will cherry-pick the theory and make use of a few crucial elements.

The Market Profile is a novel and insightful analysis of the marketplace. It includes a wealth of topics. Key among them are:

- Clarifies participant roles in the market: There are short-term participants and "Other" long-term participants, with the volume activity of the Others able to dramatically move prices. The idea is, of course, that the smaller participants (those reading this text, for example) recognize the activity of the Others and find a way to ride their coat-tails.
- Categorizes trading day-types: Non-trend, Normal, Neutral, Double-Distribution, Trend. The trader who can identify the day-type will be better able to navigate the trading day. For example, don't sell a rallying Trend Day and look to fade[1] a Neutral Day (otherwise referred to as "rotational").
- Develops a price structure model as a function of a session's first hour price range, termed Initial Balance (IB), the day's mode price, termed Point of Control (POC), and the first standard deviation in price distribution, termed Value Area, (VA). Examples from the price structure include using a POC as a pivot price (a price that can act as support or resistance) and the expectation that a Neutral market will often trade within the Value Area.
- Classifies trading mentality as initiative and responsive and refines session opening activity.
- Incorporates volume studies.

Since a picture is worth a thousand words, charts help illustrate some of these ideas. The first chart is a Market Profile view of the ES contract in early February 2009.

The Market Profile makes use of a unique presentation of price charts. Every 30 minutes of the trading session a new "time-price opportunity" (TPO) is added. In the original Market Profile, these were capitalized letters, often O, Y, Z, A, B, C, D, E, F, G, H, I, J. A TradeStation chart uses color-coded lettering, which can appear as small, colored rectangles in multiple day charts. All price levels during a given 30 minute period

---

[1] To "fade the market" is to take a position in the opposite direction of recent market price action. It is a contrarian position that is looking for a reversal in price to occur. As an example, if the ES contract has been rallying from 840.00 and approaching 850.00, then a fade at 850.00 would be a short position with an execution price near 850.00. A "resting" limit order is placed in the market ahead of the actual price reaching the desired entry price.

are drawn into a price distribution curve that, like typical price charts, has price on the vertical (right-hand) axis of the chart, but with the entire day drawn in one vertical price distribution curve. From this price distribution chart we can see how many times the market repeated trading at a given price level and we can see how price moved to new price levels with or without retracement.

Rapid price level changes which leave a single price entry are referred to as "single prints" and will show up as single letters, or in the chart shown here, a single, thin colored entry.

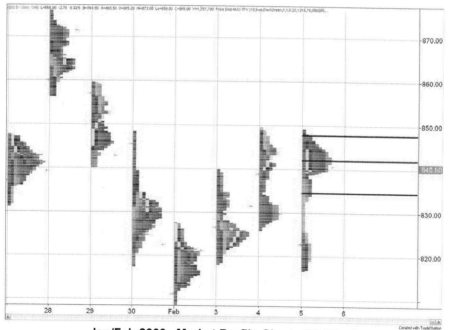

Jan/Feb 2009. Market Profile Chart. ES 30-min

The Market Profile chart is novel. If the reader is unsure of its interpretation, there will be further examples. (The Market Profile price distribution chart is achieved in TradeStation using the ActivityBar indicator.)

In the above chart, three solid lines are drawn using a custom indicator over the last day's price distribution (February 5, 2009). The middle line is the day's mode price (most frequent price) and referred to as the Point of Control (POC). The outer two lines demarcate a 70% price distribution value as defined by the Market Profile, and these correspond to one standard deviation of price distribution. This price range is referred to as the day's Value Area (VA), with the upper price line the Value Area High (VAH) and the lower price line the Value Area Low (VAL). One of the Market Profile assumptions is that price will tend to stay within the VA and extensions outside the VA indicate new price discovery and/or activity by the Other participants. The reader can imagine trading strategies that make use of this view of price.

[A note about the intra-day price charts in this book. The charts were produced using the TradeStation desktop. The great majority of them have a time axis based on the Pacific time zone (NYSE Open = 6:30am; NYSE Close = 1:00pm), as I live on the west coast of the United States. Furthermore, TradeStation will not inter-mix time zone data feeds, so that if one is charting a CME contract (Central time zone) against a NYSE data feed (Eastern time zone), one needs to specify a local time display for the two. Thus the use of Pacific time, again.]

The next chart shows the ES contract on a traditional 3-minute chart for the same day (February 5, 2009). The importance of this chart is the Initial Balance (IB) that is drawn as a solid dark line. The IB is the first hour's trading range. The IB High (IBH) and the IB Low (IBL) are the first hour's high and low prices. As with the VA distribution, the IB can be used as a baseline against which to trade. For example, the IBL and IBH can be faded (enter long at the IBL or short from the IBH). A narrow IB can be considered as price congestion and so price extensions above or below the IB can be traded as breakouts. The terminology IB Range Extension (IB RE) is used to describe such price action.

The day's IB can be compared against an historical IB, say the average IB of the last 100 trading days. Then one can speak of a wide IB or a narrow IB. Wide IBs are better candidates for price rotation; narrow IBs are better candidates for price extensions; i.e., breakouts. The narrower horizontal line, also drawn using a custom indicator, is shown along with the wider daily IB, and gives the historical IB of the last 100 trading days.

In the two charts below, from January 2nd and 20th, we see relatively narrow IBs and might expect IB RE as a result. This is in fact what occurred shortly after the first hour of trading.

An important aspect of The Market Profile, which we shall make regular use of, is the Day-Type classification. Here we review The Market Profile day-types with the help of traditional price charts.

The two charts from January 2nd and January 20th show Trend Days. Trend Days exhibit continuous selling or buying. Entering a Trend Day on a retracement to a 20-EMA (20 period Exponential Moving Average) on a 3-minute chart is one means of trading a Trend Day. Getting on the wrong side of a trend day is one of the worst ways to damage an account. If nothing else, it should be the goal of the day-trader to stay off the wrong side of a Trend Day[2]. Later we will see a tool to help identify Trend Days.

February 5, 2009. Initial Balance. ES 3-min

---

[2] Scalpers may argue they can profitably scalp Trend Days, shorting local price maxima.

January 2, 2009. Trend Day Up. ES 3-min

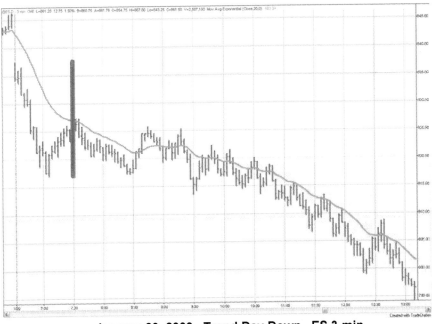

January 20, 2009. Trend Day Down. ES 3-min

The next chart, May 30, 2008, shows a Non-Trend Day. These are directionless trading days with small price range. Non-Trend Days might precede an important event, for example an FOMC announcement (Federal Reserve Open Market Committee interest rate announcement), when traders are waiting for news. With the recent stock market volatility of 2008-09, Non-Trend Days have been rare. It is often best to simply not trade during Non-Trend Days or Non-Trend Day-like periods.

The price chart from January 14, 2009 shows a Market Profile day-type referred to as a Normal Day. Normal Days do not occur as regularly as their name implies. A Normal Day occurs when the market moves to a new price level, based on economic news[3] or other fundamental factors, and then stays at the new level. It indicates a new price equilibrium and in that sense represents what we would "normally" expect the market to do: Find a next price level based on economic forces at play and then confirm it by trading around that level.

May 30, 2008. Non-Trend Day. ES 3-min

---

[3] The best free site I know for a good presentation of the economic reports calendar is http://fidweek.econoday.com.

January 14, 2009. Normal Day. ES 3-min

The Market Profile defines a Neutral Day as a day that tests both highs and lows, with rotation across the day's extremes. Neutral Days can exhibit significant volatility for the day-trader as the market trades back and forth across the day's trading range. A Neutral Day that closes to the high side of the day's range is considered more bullish than one that closes to the low side. The January 8th chart shows a bullish Neutral Day. Many day-traders enjoy trading Neutral Days because of the opportunities to fade price extremes. Reversal days, when the market makes a sudden reversal from rally to sell-off or sell-off to rally, are often characterized as Neutral. The December 29, 2008 chart shows a Neutral Day with reversal.

The last Market Profile day-type is the Double Distribution Day. This day is characterized by the market spending a significant amount of time at two different price levels. The February 4, 2009 price chart shows a Double Distribution Day. Immediately following that chart is a Market Profile price distribution chart. From this second chart it is clear how the Double Distribution identification arose. The range between the two distinct price distributions can represent intra-day support or resistance levels that the trader can use.

January 8, 2009. Neutral Day. ES 3-min

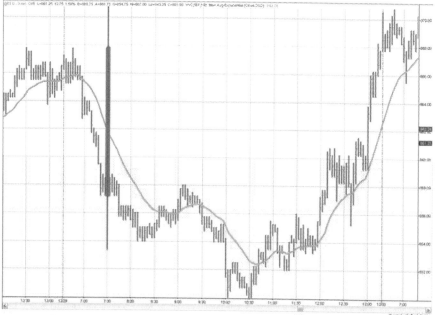

December 29, 2008. Neutral Day with Reversal. ES 3-min

February 4, 2009. Double Distribution Day. ES 3-min

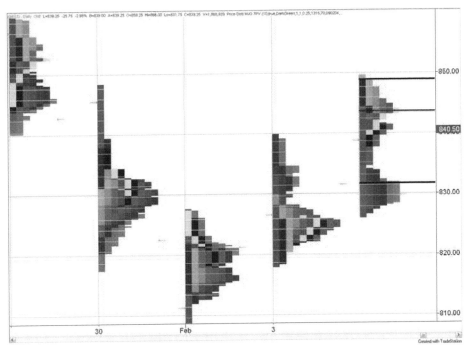

February 4, 2009. Double Distribution Day. ES 30-min

Later sections of the text will make reference to the Market Profile day-type. The reader might want to review his own charts, using various intra-day intervals, to become comfortable with day-type classification.

Market Internal Data

As mentioned in the previous chapter, one of the unique aspects of trading stock index futures is the wealth of information available about the aggregate trading of stocks. Examples abound. Data on the number of advancing stocks to the number of declining stocks; the number of stocks making new 52-week highs and lows; advance/decline ratios, and those ratios combined with their respective volumes; the number of up-ticking to down-ticking stocks — these are typical of what is referred to as Market Internal Data. One of the purest data items available is exchange-wide tick data, referred to as Ticks.

Ticks are not the single, or grouped, up- and down-tick values or trades of an individual stock or other asset[4], but a periodic exchange-wide count of the number of stocks that have traded up (the bid price moved up to the ask price to complete the last trade) minus the number of stocks that have traded down (the ask price moved down to the bid price to complete the last trade)[5]. In this way, Ticks capture periodic snapshots of the bullishness or bearishness of the market. For the NYSE, one typically sees the Ticks range between 1000 and -1000.

A number of day-trading systems make use of the Ticks to fade the market on a short-term or scalping basis. For example, if Ticks are suddenly above 1000 or below -1000, then scalpers will fade (1000 → Sell; -1000 → Buy) assuming a short-term over-bought or over-sold condition is occurring. This is shown in the following chart from February 11th where a short position was taken when Ticks were above 800 and a long position when Ticks were below -1000.

While the Ticks fade strategy is a viable scalping technique, the system defined in this book is often looking for longer-term intra-day positions. In particular, it will attempt to retain some number of open contracts in

---

[4] See the many tick charts used in the book.
[5] See the section Market Price Action for a detailed description of market bid-ask behavior.

hopes of achieving a winning runner. For this purpose, Ticks scalping is not appropriate and we use a different approach.

The e-mini stock index futures day-trading system makes use of the Ticks in a somewhat novel fashion. It computes an accumulation of 1-minute sampled Ticks from the NYSE and compares accumulations with historical intra-day values. An individual Ticks value is defined as the mean of the High, Low and Close values of a 1-minute Ticks chart[6].

The Ticks accumulation, referred to as the Cumulative Ticks, or CTs, are used to help define day-type. From the day-type determination, and using price levels and other techniques, a trading system is developed.

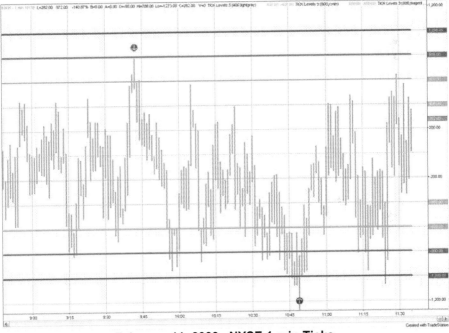

February 11, 2009. NYSE 1-min Ticks

---

[6] Research showed the following calculations gave the same relative measure of stock market activity:
- 1-minute sums of all received Ticks (based on a 1-tick chart).
- 1-minute means of all received Ticks (based on a 1-tick chart).
- 1-minute High, Low and Close mean (based on a 1-minute chart).

To aid in the interpretation of the CTs they are compared with historical CTs data. As always, a picture is worth a thousand words.

The next chart shows the way CTs are graphed. The CTs are shown as a line (dotted in a high resolution view, with one dot equal to one minute of accumulation) that overlays a 1-minute ES price chart. In the chart below, also from February 11, 2009, the CTs line meanders to the downside. On the day of this chart, one might expect a rotational market with a selling bias and look to short at a local maximum, for example the day's previous high.

A histogram at the bottom of the display gives the 1-minute Ticks accumulated by the indicator. The right-hand axis of the histogram is updated with real-time Ticks data (up to one reading per second).

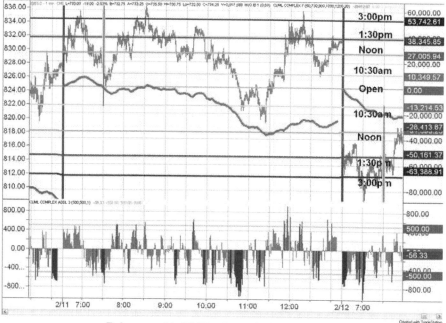

February 11, 2009. Cumulative Ticks (CTs)

There are nine horizontal lines that are part of the CTs chart. The middle horizontal line is the CTs zero, or open, line and used as a reference level. The horizontal lines, both above and below the zero line are time-of-day pivots where the CTs are averaged over the last 50 trading days (the number of trading days and the specific time-of-day pivot times are input parameters to the indicator).

The time-of-day pivots used are[7]:

- 10:30am (Completion of first hour)
- Noon (Lunch hour)
- 1:30pm (Afternoon pivot – mid-way between noon and the beginning of the last hour)
- 3:00pm (Beginning of the last hour)

There are reference pivots for bullish days – the pivot time-of-day lines above the zero line when the CTs average finished above zero, and reference pivots for bearish days – the pivot time-of-day lines below the zero line when the CTs average finished below zero. As the CTs are collected over the averaging period, counters are maintained to track values at the time-of-day pivots. Then, for any given trading day, as the day's CTs are collected they can be compared with the historical averages – the CTs values reached on average for the four time-of-day pivots. By comparing the current session CTs behavior with the time-of-day pivot averages, we are able to estimate the day-type as it unfolds.

Using the above chart from February 11, 2009, we see the CTs were fairly neutral to slightly bearish – neither bulls nor bears were in control. We refer to this as "Equivocal CTs." When this occurs, we do not expect a Trend Day and the market can, generally, be faded from price level extrema. Note that it took until 2:30pm NYSE (11:30am Pacific) to reach the average negative Noon NYSE reading. After which there was something of a rally with the CTs turning up. It was a Neutral day.

CTs examples will help clarify how the indicator is used. The next chart, from January 2, 2009, shows what is termed "Unequivocal CTs." There is little doubt that this is an extremely strong Trend Day up. During this session the day-trader typically does not attempt shorts but looks to get long through some price retracement technique.

---

[7] Time-of-Day Pivots are given in NYSE time. The underlying price chart is based on local time (Pacific in my case).

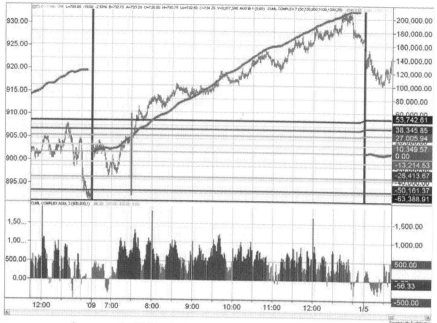

January 2, 2009. Unequivocal CTs – Trend Day Up

January 2, 2009. ES 3-min

The next CTs chart from January 20, 2009, shows another Unequivocal CTs session, this time a Trend Day down. The comments made about the previous chart apply, but now to the short side.

These last two charts are straightforward in their interpretation and fairly rare in that regard. In general, it will be more difficult to so easily discern how to use the CTs. But they are, nonetheless, an invaluable view of the trading day.

The next example from February 9, 2009, shows an Equivocal CTs chart. The day turned out to be Neutral and the trader could fade both local maxima and minima price levels.

The example from January 22, 2009, shows a "Reversal CTs" chart. This was a Neutral day and with a strong afternoon reversal. This is a difficult session to trade. One approach was to enter short after the reversal rally became exhausted (here interestingly, after the opening gap down was filled). Again, specific trade strategy and setups will be presented later in the book in order to help manage a reversal such as this.

Referring back to the February 11, 2009, CTs chart, which consisted of Equivocal and bearish CTs, we expect the day to unfold as Neutral. A trade strategy that developed late in the day was to short the market on a return to the day's previous high. The Equivocal CTs supported this setup. A limit order to short from 831.75 was a well-planned trade.

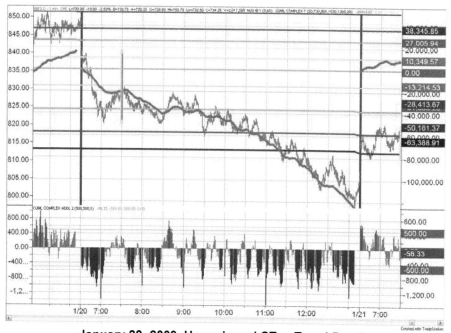

January 20, 2009. Unequivocal CTs –Trend Day Down

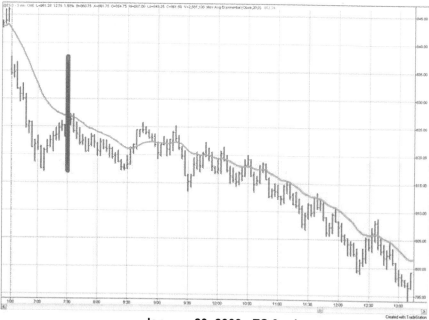

January 20, 2009. ES 3-min

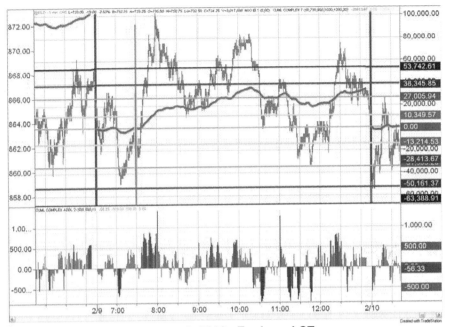

February 9, 2009. Equivocal CTs

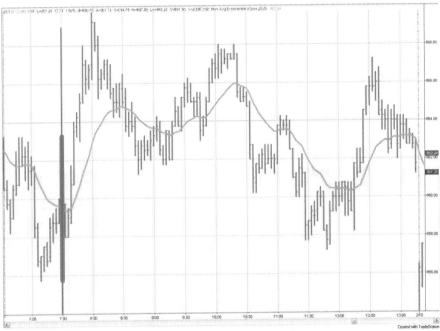

February 9, 2009. ES 3-min

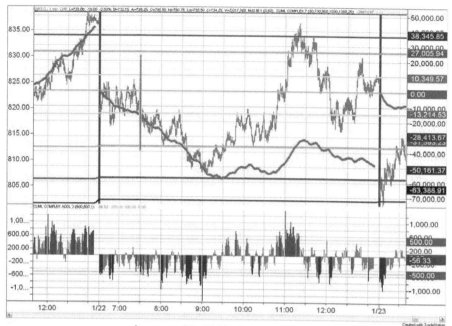

January 22, 2009. Reversal CTs

January 22, 2009. Neutral Day (Reversal). ES 3-min

February 11, 2009. ES 3-min

The time-of-day CT pivots are used as guidelines: There is no single indicator that supplies a black and white reading of the market. If the CTs are not reaching their time-of-day pivots, then they can be considered Equivocal. It is generally easier to say when the CTs are Unequivocal and part of a strong trend.

Traders are continually trying to answer the age-old question: Are we trending or not? CTs help answer this question and are an important tool to tell us how *not* to trade; i.e., to help us from trading against a trend. The trader should not be positioned on the wrong side of Unequivocal CTs. Equivocal CTs will indicate that rotation is expected and we are to look for key price levels against which to trade. Equivocal CTs will indicate it is unlikely we will see an extraordinarily strong trend develop and profit targets can be adjusted accordingly.

Because nothing can predict the future, and because daily stock market activity can take sudden swings, it is important to be prepared for intra-day changes in CTs. The histogram of current 1-minute Ticks readings can be used to watch for reversals. A sharp and continuous orientation change in histogram values (minus to plus; plus to minus) can indicate a change is afoot. The chart below shows a trading day with a strong reversal in the last hour. The section on Time-of-Day Patterns covers material to help alert the trader to the fact that last hour reversals are not infrequent and need to be comprehended by a trading system.

Because CTs are a direct and unfiltered reading of stock market activity they are an important trading tool.

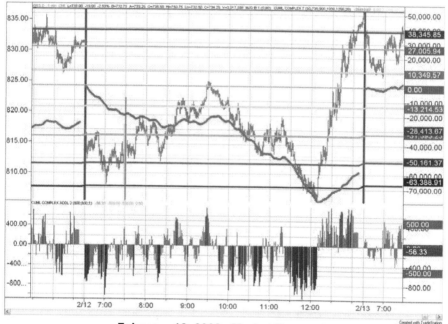

February 12, 2009. Market Reversal

CTs-Price Divergence

The Cumulative Ticks (CTs) are an accurate measure of underlying stock market activity. That is not to say that a CTs reading cannot precipitously change orientation and reverse course, because that is the intra-day nature of the stock market. But in general, the indicator is a good guide in assisting with day-type determination.

When watching CTs and futures prices together there is a relationship that the day-trader may be able to use. It is referred to as *CTs-Price Divergence*. As with the more traditional *Inter-Market Divergence* (see the section later in this chapter) we are looking for discrepancies from normal market performance that can be exploited for profitable trades. In the case of CTs-Price Divergence, this is a discrepancy between NYSE Ticks and CME ES futures price. As always, a picture is worth a thousand words.

Referring to the CTs chart from March 9, 2009, below, we see an Equivocally bearish day in-progress, and then between 10:15 and 11:15 AM (Pacific) a CTs-Price divergence occurs:

- CTs are flat
- ES price rises 9 points from 676 to 685

This is highlighted with a rectangle surrounding the flat[8] CTs period (the histogram) and a trend line under the ES price rise. The divergence is not short-term by intra-day standards, lasting more than 30 minutes.

The divergence points to one of two possible conditions:

1. We are in the midst of a reversal, or
2. The ES price rise is divergent from broader stock market activity and cannot be supported.

Reversals are typically accompanied with a clear change in the CTs orientation, so it is determined that the first possibility is not accurate. We appear to be in the midst of a CTs-Price Divergence which represents a trading opportunity.

---

[8] It is the summation of 1-minute tick averages over a fixed duration that is flat.

The reader may ask: How can such a divergence even be possible, because there never are wide price differences between the cash and futures markets (if there were, the arbitrage opportunity would quickly be closed by those seeking to exploit it)? The answer is that the ES price is not divergent from its underlying index value but from the recent sum of the broader NYSE Ticks – in some sense, a mixed market condition. This discrepancy cannot continue for long.

Referring again to the March 9th chart, because the CTs have remained Equivocally bearish a short entry is the goal. We wait until after the 1:00-2:00pm afternoon rally period and using a price retracement to the previous 682-684 support area (support becomes resistance), a short from 683 makes for a profitable trade. Many more examples of this kind of trading will be covered in the book.

The second CTs-Price Divergence example is from March 6, 2009. In the second chart, we see two divergences. The first is similar to the March 9th case, where a flat CTs reading coincides with an eight point ES price rise. Again, this divergence points to ES futures prices that the broader market cannot sustain. A second divergence appears around 9:30am Pacific when a falling CTs reading coincides with a flat futures price. Both these divergences represent trading opportunities. There will be additional examples of this style of trading in the Trade Setups chapter.

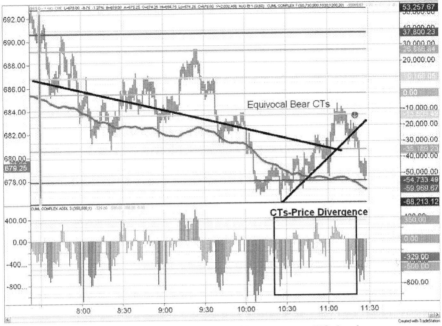

March 9, 2009. CTs-Price Divergence. ES 1-min

March 6, 2009. CTs-Price Divergence. ES 1-min

Price Levels

The trading system makes use of price levels to enter and exit the market. Traditional price level definitions are augmented with Market Profile defined levels and prioritized to help make trading decisions.

Most, if not all, serious traders make use of price levels in their trading. Again, it is a combination of techniques which defines the system. Price Level analysis is one of the important techniques.

The chart below, December 3, 2008, shows the price levels that will be used in the trading system. These levels are standard within the trading community and their definitions (see below) are well-known and widely used.

December 3, 2008. Price Levels. ES 3-min

The price levels are defined as:

- PDH = Previous Day's High
- PDL = Previous Day's Low
- PDC = Previous Day's Close
- Pivot = (PDH + PDL + PDC) / 3
- Open = Today's Opening Price
- R1 = (2 * Pivot) – PDL (Resistance Level 1)
- S1 = (2 * Pivot) – PDH (Support Level 1)
- R2 = (Pivot – S1) + R1   (Resistance Level 2)
- S2 = Pivot – (R1 – S1)   (Support Level 2)
- IB = First hour's trading range
- IBH = IB High
- IBL = IB Low

Some traders also use R3 (Resistance Level 3) and S3 (Support Level 3) and Mid-point levels between the Pivot and R1, R1 and R2, the Pivot and S1, S1 and S2 (e.g., Mid-P-R1 = (P + R1) / 2), etc. Practice shows these levels are not as reliable and/or make for overly cluttered charts.

In addition to these price levels, which can be drawn by software at the session open (the IB values must wait for the first hour, of course), the trader is required to maintain price levels that are generated during the day's trading session. This includes: Day's Previous High and Low (DPH/L) and Local price maximums and minimums (local extrema).

The next chart, December 12, 2008, shows how the trader maintains markings of the day's previous high price. Later, we will see how, if the day-type supports it, shorting at the day's previous high can be a valid trade setup, when used with the correct profit-target scale-out and stop-loss protection.

December 12, 2008. Intra-Day Local Price Extrema. ES 3-min

The different price levels covered so far are prioritized by importance in day-trade setups, in the following highest-to-lowest priority order:

1. DPH, DPL, Local Extrema
2. IB, IBH, IBL
3. PDH, PDL
4. Pivot, Open
5. R1, S1
6. R2, S2

The Trade Setups chapter will detail how these price levels are used to trade.

Big Numbers

If one watches the market intra-day on a regular basis, then it becomes clear that trading occurs around "big numbers," referred to here as BNs.

Not only do short-term scalpers make use of BNs, but large institutional investors, looking to buy and sell in volume throughout the day, and using high-frequency trade automation, make use of BNs to make trading decisions. In this way, the stock market and stock index futures play off each other.

As an example of how BNs are used throughout the day, consider an ES 750 level (February 23, 2009 charts, below). The 750 value may be considered a BN. If the market is in the midst of a sell-off and moves below the 750 BN, then a retracement back to 750 might be used by traders to complete additional sales. If selling is the goal, then a retracement to that BN is a good place to sell, based on the initial breakout below it. Later, tests back to 750 will be closely watched. If the market can exceed the level, then a further rally above might be expected. However, if the market struggles to get back above 750, one might conclude price will reverse and again trade lower.

In the ES contract, there is a two point BN phenomenon: The market will often test BN price levels using approximately two points of price discovery, and the e-mini day-trader needs to be aware of this. Consider the two charts from February 23, 2009. The first shows a two point price discovery at the 750 BN. The market moved down to 748.25 before finding support and reversing. It is as if the market gave itself two points to determine that 750 would support it, at least temporarily. The second chart, later in the same day, shows selling down through the 750 level to 744, followed by two retracements back up to the 750 level. In the second attempt, price did not complete a full retracement but turned back at 748.50. Obviously the two point value is an approximate rule-of-thumb.

While the reader might first view BNs incredulously (I certainly did – How can any particular round number have an effect on something as vast and diverse as the stock market?), the day-trader must at least be on the look out for BN values and be aware when he or she is trading around them. Stop-loss price levels may need to take into consideration the two point discovery phenomenon. See the Trade Examples chapter for additional charts highlighting Big Numbers and key price levels.

February 23, 2009 (1). ES BN Two Point Phenomenon. ES Ticks

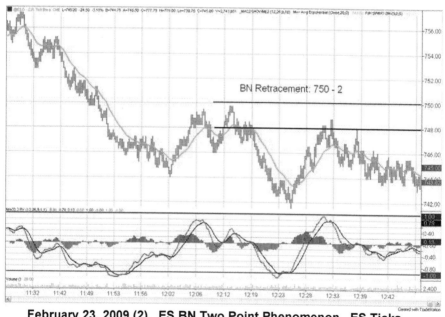

February 23, 2009 (2). ES BN Two Point Phenomenon. ES Ticks

Inter-Day Price Levels

In addition to short-term intra-day price levels, the trader must also be aware of inter-day price levels that define longer-term support and resistance. These are created from previous session activity. Often, important inter-day support and resistance and BNs are coincident.

The Market Profile chart view can be used to spot important inter-day price levels. These price levels do not have a simple formula as in the intra-day cases (Pivot, R1, S1, etc.) [9] but are based on previous support and resistance levels and gaps.

In the next chart, a Market Profile view from late January to early February 2009, we see an intermediate-term price level in the ES contract at 875. This level is important for two reasons:

- The market first tested the price on January 28th. The second test back to that level, which occurred on February 9th, must be carefully watched for a re-test failure or successful breakout.
- 875 may be considered a BN.

In this example, when intra-day signals support entering short from the 875 price level, then the inter-day price relevancy of 875 adds weight to a trade entry decision.

From the same Market Profile chart another key price level can be seen. This is the price gap that occurred between January 27th and 28th (see the small square marked "Gap"), and which was closed beginning on January 29th ("Filling the Gap"). The trader who is aware of the gap from 855, and notices weakness at that level, can take advantage of knowledge that an inter-day gap is in the process of filling.

---

[9] Some traders make use of weekly Pivot, S1/2 and R1/2 values.

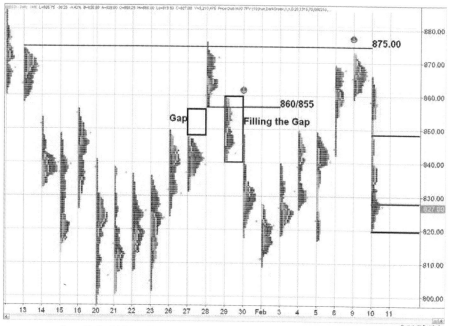

Jan-Feb 2009. Market Profile Inter-Day Price. ES 30-min

Resistance Becomes Support (RBS) and Support Becomes Resistance (SBR)

When key price levels are exceeded then their role in the price support/resistance dynamics of the market can reverse. That is, a price level that was once resistance will become support and vice versa – a price level that was once support will become resistance. The RBS acronym is used for the bullish case – Resistance Becomes Support, and SBR is used for the bearish case – Support Becomes Resistance.

The trader can take advantage of this phenomenon to define high probability trades. As always, a picture is worth a thousand words.

In the next chart, from April 16, 2009, the Previous Day's High (PDH) is 850.50, and 850 is clearly a Big Number. Between 7:00 and 9:00am (Pacific) we see the market make three separate attempts to exceed the 850 level, before finally breaching it in a fourth attempt. After exceeding 850, the market briefly extends up to approximately 854.

Now, with the key 850 level exceeded, that price level becomes support, and what was once resistance is now support. At this point the trader will carefully watch price action for retracement back down to the 850 level, because that level may now offer new support that can be incorporated in a trade.

Should the market retrace back to 850, consolidate there and not move lower, then 850 can make an excellent long entry. The trader will look for confirming signals that will give additional confidence to a long position. For example, are CTs Bullish? Has the market been consolidating over the lunch hour for a possible afternoon rally attempt? The new 850 support level can become a powerful jumping off point for an afternoon rally. In fact, that is what happened.

The reader may be thinking, It's is all a bit too vague, the notion that a fixed price point could be so important. Not really, though. What the market is telling us is that with the breach of the 850 level, price has moved to a new plateau and it is ready to stay above the old level. Thus when a retracement back to the old resistance/new support level holds, we might expect the market to move higher[10].

The experienced trader will be able to transition his view of key price levels from support to resistance and vice versa, based on price action. It requires carefully watching the market around key price levels. As always, there are no hard and fast rules in predicting what the market will do. But there are higher probability outcomes, given a recent history of price.

---

[10] The reader who is familiar with the fascinating Nicolas Darvas story, How I Made $2,000,000 in the Stock Market, 1960, might recall that we have described a "Darvas Box" in the example here.

April 16, 2009. 850 Resistance Becomes Support. ES 3-Min

Price Extension and Retracement

At this point the reader may be able to discern key aspects of the trading system. A cornerstone of the system is to differentiate the day-type as not a Trend Day (Neutral, Normal, Double Distribution) or a Trend Day and trade accordingly. If not a Trend Day, then the market is faded based on a predetermined price level and following some price extension. If a Trend Day, then local price retracement is used to enter in the direction of the trend. This section covers the next two aspects of the trading system: Price Extension and Retracement.

Price Extension

Price Extension implies fading the market when its price has been extended too far in one direction. In this regard, the market is viewed as a rubber band that is continuously stretched and relaxed. If we can determine levels at which the market is sufficiently stretched and may revert to a mean equilibrium, then we can develop a viable trading program. Price extended to the upside is often referred to as an overbought market. Price extended to the downside is often referred to as an oversold market. Price levels, described in the previous section, are an important tool in determining price extension. Technical indicators are another.

There are two broad classes of technical indicator that can be used to determine price extension: Oscillators and Moving Average indicators. A familiar oscillator is the Stochastic. A familiar moving average indicator is the Moving Average Convergence Divergence (MACD or "Mac-D"). The Stochastic, which was the work of George Lane and dates from the 1950s, is sometimes classified as a leading indicator because it is self-referencing: Current prices are compared with a range of previous prices to give a relative measure of price extension. The MACD, which was the work of Gerald Appel and dates from the 1960s, is sometimes classified as a trailing indicator because it is based on moving average price calculations, where the averaging of previous prices inherently introduces some lag.

Because the Stochastic creates a signal line by averaging its computed prices, and because in practice it is actually difficult to see the MACD as necessarily lagging the Stochastic, it is unclear if this leading/trailing classification is that relevant to the day-trader. A chart of the ES contract with both Stochastic and MACD indicators is shown below (February 14, 2009; MACD top indicator, Stochastic below).

Whichever indicator is used, the trader must be aware that they do not provide much information when the market is trending and persists in an overbought or oversold condition. Importantly, the technical indicators are used to confirm price extension and do not, by themselves, provide a complete trading signal.

Because the MACD has proved to be a reliable indicator for price extension when used with other techniques, it is the technical indicator used in the remainder of the text.

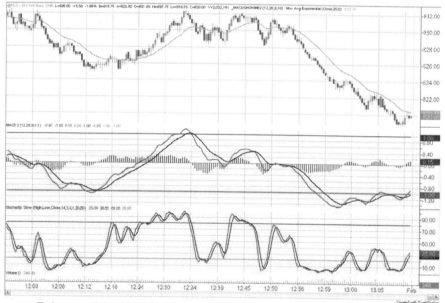

February 14, 2009. MACD and Stochastic Indicators. ES Ticks

MACD

I have found the MACD to be one of the most useful technical indicators. While many technical indicators are at first somewhat confusing, once an indicator's constituent parts are broken down and studied individually it becomes clear what exactly is being graphed. A trader needs to know exactly how his or her indicators function in order to make best use of them and, importantly, so as not to oversubscribe their use.

The MACD is a comparison of two Exponential Moving Averages (EMA)[11] of different lengths, what are referred to as the Fast MA and the Slow MA. The Fast MA will more closely follow actual price and it will pull away from the Slow MA when the market makes a move. By comparing the difference between the Fast MA and the Slow MA one gets an indication for how fast the market is moving and then when that move has begun to slow. The process of a market moving rapidly in one direction and then slowing can indicate price extension and exhaustion of the extension.

The first figure below shows the Fast MA and Slow MA plotted on an ES tick chart. Below the ES price chart is a curve that is the difference between the Fast MA and the Slow MA. This difference is the first component of the MACD. Where the Fast MA has pulled away from the Slow MA to the upside the MACD is positive. Where the Fast MA has pulled away from the Slow MA to the downside the MACD is negative. Where the Fast MA and Slow MA are identical and cross, the MACD is zero.

Inspection of price charts for a given bar interval and MACD parameters will give an approximate maximum difference in the Fast and Slow MAs. In the case of the ES chart, using a 12-period Fast MA and a 26-period Slow MA, a Fast MA-Slow MA difference of 1.0 (which is one ES point) is

---

[11] The EMA is an example of what computer programmers call a "recursive function": The next term in the calculation is defined using the previous one. The calculation for the nth term is: $EMA_n = \lambda * EMA_{n-1} + (1 - \lambda) * Value_n \rightarrow$ Add the previous value of the EMA, EMA_{n-1}, to the next data value, $Value_n$. The previous value of the EMA and the next value are weighted by λ; for example, $\lambda = 0.90$ gives a 90% weight to the EMA value and a 10% weight to the data value. Set $EMA_0 = Value_1$ and work forward to see why "exponential" is used to describe the calculation. Then, as an example, $EMA_3 = \lambda^2 * Value_1 + \lambda * (1 - \lambda) * Value_2 + (1 - \lambda) * Value_3$. The λ weight becomes an exponential term.

marked as an overbought/oversold watermark with horizontal lines used at these levels.

The next component of the MACD indicator is a moving average of the Fast MA and Slow MA difference. The average of the MACD difference will smooth the Fast MA minus Slow MA difference line and create a "signal line." When the MACD crosses its signal line one assumes the orientation of the Fast MA and Slow MA is beginning to change (e.g., Fast MA above Slow MA to Fast MA below Slow MA). It is this change which can indicate completion of a price extension.

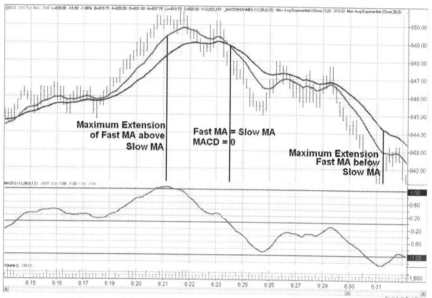

February 10, 2009 MACD. Fast-Slow MA. ES Ticks

Finally, the complete MACD indicator display includes a histogram of the difference between the MACD and the MACD average lines. The complete MACD indicator is shown in the next figure. Two points where the MACD and its average are identical, so that its histogram value is zero, are shown.

The MACD is often described with inputs: MACD (F, S, SL) where F is the Fast MA period; S is the Slow MA period; and SL is the signal line MA period. MACD(12, 26, 9) is the default configuration used here.

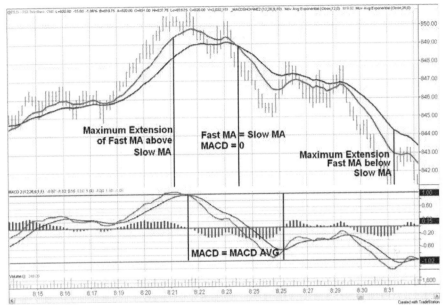

February 10, 2009 MACD. Complete Indicator. ES Ticks

A *MACD-Price Divergence* is a good technical indication of possible price extension exhaustion. There are both Buy MACD-Price Divergences and Sell MACD-Price Divergences:

- Buy: MACD is moving upward from Oversold while Price is not making new lows.
- Sell: MACD is moving downward from Overbought while Price is not making new highs.

See the next two charts (February 10th and 13th). Buy and Sell entries are shown with arrows. Note that trade entries are made on retracement to a 20-EMA line.

MACD-Price Divergence trades are covered in the Trade Setups chapter.

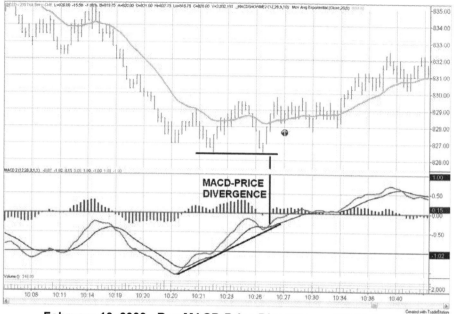

February 10, 2009. Buy MACD-Price Divergence. ES Ticks

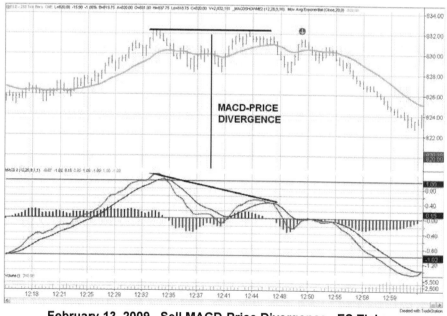

February 13, 2009. Sell MACD-Price Divergence. ES Ticks

Statistical MACD

As just described, the MACD outputs the difference between two exponential moving averages. The moving averages are based on the price of the underlying asset. In this case, using similar 5-minute bar charts, an overbought/oversold (OB/OS) MACD level might be 8 ticks (2 points) for the S&P 500 e-mini ES contract and five ticks ($0.05) for INTC shares.

Using the MACD across a variety of assets and time-frames requires the trader figure OB/OS levels for each application, which can be tedious and error-prone. The 1st Edition of the book contained tables of MACD overbought and oversold settings that varied across the four key e-mini stock index futures (ES, NQ, TF, YM).

As a result, a technique of moving MACD software (and other similar indicators) to statistical outputs was developed. Specifically, instead of underlying prices, the new Statistical MACD outputs *z-score* values, where a z-score is a number of standard deviations a current value is from a mean value.

Technical indicators can be moved to a statistical output format in order to make them more robust. This results in indicators that can be used across markets without modification. The trading system uses *statistical indicators* in order to eliminate asset-specific settings. In this format, the indicators can be used across the four e-minis without change.

The most common method of estimating the spread, or dispersion, of a data set is standard deviation. The data's mean, or average, referred to with the Greek letter μ ("mu"), is first calculated. The data's standard deviation is then calculated as the average distance of the data set from its mean. The standard deviation, referred to with the Greek letter σ ("sigma"), is easy to work with because it takes values that are the same units as the original, underlying data.

The science of statistics has determined that for many naturally occurring populations (population height, weight, test score, etc.), data is "normally" distributed about its mean. This is the well-known bell curve of population distribution. Interestingly, bell curves are completely defined by their mean and standard deviation. This allows one to say that a normal distribution has approximately 70% of its data contained with one standard deviation of its mean and 95% within two standard deviations, etc., regardless of the values computed for the data's mean and standard deviation. For example, if test scores range from 0 to 100, with a mean of 75 and a standard deviation of 10, then we can predict that 70% of the scores range from 65 to 85 (75-10 to 75+10).

It is questionable whether financial markets can be accurately modeled using a normal distribution. Markets are said to have "fat tails," meaning there may be an unexpected amount of data far from the mean, say outside of the two, or even three, standard deviation levels. Fat tails model panics and over-exuberance, and there is a large body of financial analysis that uses different assumptions of dispersion than the normal distribution. None-the-less, normal distribution works as a good first approximation that can be used by traders. For example, the Market Profile Value Area is defined as encompassing 70% of price movement beginning from a mode (most common) price. The 70% value represents a one standard deviation variation in price.

Making use of standard deviation with price and, in particular, bar charts, is straightforward. The standard deviation of recent price history is first calculated using some number of previous bar prices. Picking a history length is similar to selecting the length for a moving average indicator. Then a standard deviation relative position of recent price can be determined. Specifically, the current price, x, is said to be at "$(x - \mu)/\sigma$ standard deviations"; that is, the current price, x, is some number of standard deviations displaced from the mean.

The value $(x - \mu)/\sigma$ may at first seem obscure. But consider the meaning of any fraction or ratio, for example, the fraction one-third, which asks, How many threes are there in one? In the same way, the ratio $(x - \mu)/\sigma$ asks, How many standard deviations are there in $x - \mu$, the distance of the current price from mean price? The technical term for the ratio $(x - \mu)/\sigma$ is z-score. By converting indicator output values to z-scores we are able to move technical indicators to a statistical basis.

The figure from March 26th show a side-by-side comparison of 5-minute ES and INTC charts with standard MACD and new statistical MACD (MACD SD) plots below the bar charts. Both MACDs input the popular (12, 26, 9) moving average length values. MACD SD takes one additional parameter, the price history length, which is used to calculate a recent MACD mean and standard deviation. In this example, price history length was set to 400 bars. The standard MACD has used an OB/OS level of 1.5 points for the ES contract and $0.05 for INTC. The statistical MACD SD uses a fixed 2-σ OB/OS level (two standard

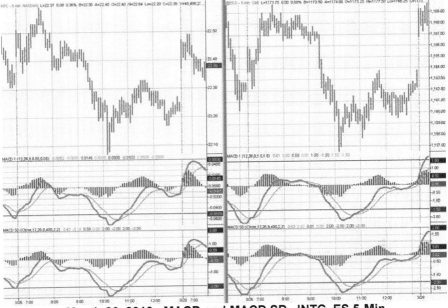

March 26, 2010. MACD and MACD SD. INTC, ES 5-Min

deviations) for both ES and INTC. The MACD SD can be moved across assets without modification.

Converting technical indicators to statistical, z-score outputs can be helpful whenever absolute prices are referenced. Another example is a price extension/compression indicator. In this case, the trader is interested in gauging the extent of recent price action in a rotational market: Has a recent move been significant enough to consider fading the market expecting some reversal in price?

One method of measuring price extension/compression calculates the "highest high – lowest low" difference of the last N bars. If the difference is greater than some average price range, the assumption is that a significant price move has occurred. But when price movement is asset-specific, the measurement is complicated when moved from one chart to the next. Just as in the case of the MACD, a statistical approach is preferred.

The indicator "Average Price Range Standard Deviation" (APR SD) has been written using the z-score techniques of standard deviation to measure price extension and compression. The December 30th chart shows the MACD SD overlaid with the APR SD on the Russell 2000 e-mini futures TF contract (NYBOT), 233-tick. APR SD produces a signal line when recent price extension is above the two standard deviation level. Price compression is indicated when the APR SD indicator is at a comparable number of negative standard deviations.

Using the MACD SD and APR SD in tandem offers the trader possible entry signals. While it must be said that this chart gives a particularly compelling illustration of the indicators, the theory, from a technical perspective, is consistent: Price extension may indicate a point of market rotation and MACD cross-over provides a reasonable entry point. Once again, there are no changes to the z-score based technical indicators when moving them to different assets.

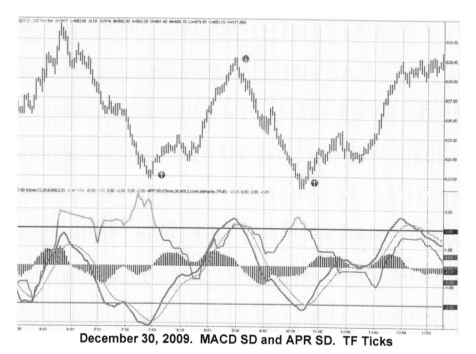

December 30, 2009. MACD SD and APR SD. TF Ticks

The general implementation of a statistical indicator is:

1. Calculate technical indicator values. This is identical to the computation used for the original technical indicator.
2. Save the technical indicator values.

3. At the close of the last bar, calculate the mean and standard deviation from the saved technical indicator values; then calculate the z-score value for the current bar.
4. Plot the z-score value similarly to how the original indicator plotted its output.

There are two points to consider when carrying out a statistical implementation:

1. When saving technical indicator values, make use of an efficient data structure to retain value history. Data arrays, which require shifting previous entries to make room for the next entry are inefficient. A queue structure that provides efficient FIFO insertion is preferred.
2. Do not compute the statistical indicator on intra-bar updates. If lengthy price histories are used for mean and standard deviation calculation, then performing their computation intra-bar can be compute intensive. Most platforms support the option of restricting indicator computation to the close of a bar, and this is adequate to avoid unnecessary computation. The minor restriction does not eliminate the use of tick charts, and statistical indicators continue to work with tick charts. For example, see the TF 233-tick chart, above.

The use of statistical indicators can standardize the discussion of trade decisions and can add discipline to a trading program. Trade entry and exit decisions begin to be based on a well-defined measure of general price action, as opposed to varied, and perhaps inaccurate, asset specific values. It's not rocket science, but it is a useful technique.

The trading system described in this book uses statistical MACD to help measure price extension. One note of caution in applying technical indicators: There are no trade setups based solely on technical indicator. Rather, the indicators are used to help guide and confirm views of recent price action. For example, an MACD-Price Divergence is not traded in isolation, but is used to help confirm a possible trade entry developed based on the additional views of the market; e.g., Day-Type, and Price Level.

Price Retracement

Price retracement can be categorized as:

- Retracement to a relative price level;
- Retracement to an absolute price level; and,
- Retracement to a local price level.

Retracement to a relative price level means price movement to a level that is relative to a previous move up or down in price. The popular Fibonacci retracement is included in this category. The first chart below, February 11, 2009, shows a short entry based on a 50% retracement in a recent price move.

Retracement to an absolute price level means price movement to one of the levels defined in the Price Levels section of the chapter. A price level, based on previous highs and lows, is determined to be significant and useful as a trading entry or exit price. The trading system uses this type of price level retracement.

Retracement to a locally defined price level means price movement to a level defined by an indicator used on local data, for example a 20-period EMA[12]. The February 5, 2009 chart shows a series of long entries based on a local pullback to the 20-EMA on a tick chart. The trading system uses this type of price level retracement. In particular, it can be a useful means of getting on a longer-term movement in price that is occurring as part of a Trend Day or as a means of entering a trade without chasing the market.

---

[12] I first came across the use of 20-EMA price retracement as a trade entry strategy in the well-known trading text, Street Smarts: High Probability Short-Term Trading Strategies, Linda Bradford Raschke (LBR) and Laurence A. Connors, 1996. There it was referred to as part of a "Holy Grail" setup. LBR is an extremely knowledgeable and well-known active trader, having been featured in New Market Wizards, Jack Schwager, 1992. Her trading site, www.lbrgroup.com, is popular among active day-traders.

February 11, 2009. Fibonacci Price Level Retracement. ES Ticks

February 5, 2009. 20-EMA Price Retracement. ES Ticks

Time-of-Day Patterns and Pivots

Watching the stock market ebb-and-flow day after day, one begins to see time-of-day patterns to the trading. Price action often exhibits predictable behavior during these periods. For example, congestion over the NYSE lunch hour followed by an afternoon rally. When price action appears to change direction at a particular time-of-day, then we refer to it as a Time-of-Day Pivot.

These time patterns and pivots can be based on well-defined events; for example, the regular release of economic reports at 10:00am (Eastern), the conclusion of the NYSE lunch-hour around 1:00pm (Eastern), or the last hour of trading beginning at 3:00pm (Eastern).

It is said that amateurs open the market and professionals close it. It is true that following the first hour of the session and in the afternoon the trader has more information to analyze the market than earlier in the day: IB and price action around the IBH and IBL; the day's highs and lows; tests of the previous day's highs and lows; and the day-type may have made itself known. In this sense, there is considerable price "architecture" in-place which can be used by the day-trader later in the trading day.

On the other hand, some traders find that getting in the market early provides the best chance of profitability, and if the day is a Trend Day, then getting on the trend early is easier, and certainly more profitable, than later trying to find an entry point. Studies show that the first hour is the most volatile, followed by the last hour. There can be considerably fewer resting limit orders in the Bid/Ask queues early in a session, which contributes to e-mini volatility.

In general, I have found trading to be more predictable after the first hour of the day session, while recognizing that a first thirty minute pivot offers good trades. Afternoon session trading can take advantage of the day's price architecture, and there is typically plenty of volatility in the last hour to make trading interesting (and frustrating!).

The Trade Setups chapter provides time-of-day guidelines to assist the day-trader and give additional form to the trading day. This helps limit the amount of time spent in front of screens.

Inter-Market Analysis

A benefit of trading the e-mini stock index futures is the contribution of four related contracts that can be traded. The ES, NQ, TF and YM (S&P 500, Nasdaq 100, Russell 2000 and DJIA) can be traded individually and by looking for discrepancies among them. Market pair techniques, popularly advocated for swing trading (intermediate term trades with positions expected to last from several days to weeks or months) can be used by the day-trader. This is similar to how, for example, gold and silver or oil and natural gas futures are traded in pairs.

The four e-mini stock index futures markets can be put into leader-follower relationships based on the composition of their underlying stock indices. One such pairing is:

Leader	TF (Russell 2000)	NQ (Nasdaq 100)
Follower	ES (S&P 500)	YM (DJIA)

The assumption to this order is that the Small Cap Russell 2000 will move more precipitously than the larger S&P 500, and the Nasdaq 100 high-tech stocks will show the similar behavior relative to the more stalwart DJIA.

In these relationships, if the TF is rallying but the ES remains in a tight trading range, then a long ES position may be warranted, based on the expectation that the ES follower will catch up to the TF leader. When other trade parameters are in-place, this type of trading can be profitable. There will be examples in the Trade Setups chapter.

In order to quickly take advantage of inter-market divergences, the day-trading system maintains a single screen view of all four markets. This is referred to as the e-mini 4-plex screen. The next chart gives an example. The 4-plex screen arranges the TF, ES and NQ, YM charts in a leader-follower format and uses a fixed time-frame 3-minute chart so that identical points in the trading day are compared. The charts include individual price level lines.

From the 4-plex example below, January 28, 2009, we see a discrepancy between the YM (Dow) contract and the other markets. The YM is lagging the other three by a considerable amount. With the YM holding to its R2 level, the ES, TF and NQ markets are well above their R2 price levels. Furthermore, this occurred on a Trend Day up, as verified by an Unequivocal CTs chart; see the second chart.

Combining the inter-market divergence, the Trend Day up indication, a 1:30pm time-of-day pivot with a low-risk "buying ledge," a YM long position at the 1:30pm pivot made for a good entry.

Becoming adept at this style of inter-market divergence day-trading requires the trader quickly survey the 4-plex screen to determine if a divergence is in-place. Because there are specific time-of-day periods when trades are considered, this type of scanning is feasible. Software can be used to provide automated alerts, as well.

In order to clarify the cases of inter-market divergence that are considered tradable, the following schematics provide templates for trade setups. There may be others, but the first two shown here are fairly easy to identify and give the most reliable setups. The short side is shown; the long side is similar and in the opposite direction.

A second type of inter-market divergence trading is based on a longer-term inter-day analysis of the market. As with the 3-minute e-mini 4-plex chart of intra-day price, the four key stock index markets (the cash markets) are displayed on a single screen, using daily charts. Here the trader is looking for leader-follower behavior that can be used in day-trading. An example best illustrates the concept.

The daily chart from the Fall-Winter 2008-09 period, below, is a daily 4-plex view. Included in the charts are 50- and 200-Day MAs (Moving Averages) and a horizontal price level that is the year's opening price for the index. Generally, if the market is above the year's opening price, then we have a bull market; if the market is below the year's opening price, then we have a bear market. In any case, the trader, in his preparation for a day-trading session, scans the daily 4-plex charts and looks for inter-market divergences.

From recent daily charts one can see a clear discrepancy between the Nasdaq 100 Index and the other three indices (SP 500, Russell 2000, DJIA). The Nasdaq 100 (upper right quadrant) is above its year's opening price and at its highs for the year. The other markets are below their year's opening price and, in the case of the Dow (lower right quadrant) showing a series of recent lower highs, which is bearish. The day-trader will make use of this information.

January 28, 2009. E-Mini 4-Plex Screen View. 3-min

January 28, 2009. Unequivocal CTs. Trend Day Up

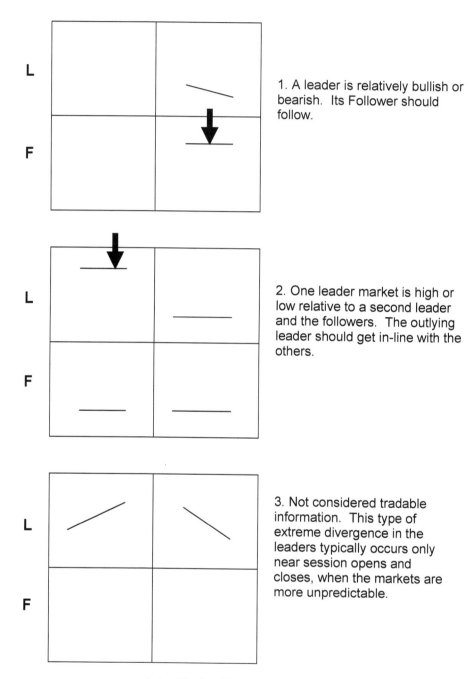

1. A leader is relatively bullish or bearish. Its Follower should follow.

2. One leader market is high or low relative to a second leader and the followers. The outlying leader should get in-line with the others.

3. Not considered tradable information. This type of extreme divergence in the leaders typically occurs only near session opens and closes, when the markets are more unpredictable.

Inter-Market Divergence Schematics

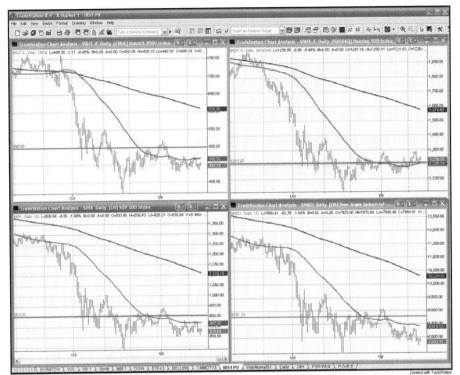

Fall-Winter 2008-09. Stock Indices Daily 4-Plex View

For example, if the NQs are *not* showing strength on the day, we will be looking for short setups, and especially with the YM e-mini, as the DJIA is showing particular weakness. Again, the Nasdaq 100 is bullish divergent from the other markets, so that if during an up-coming trading session it is showing weakness, we might expect significant weakness in the follower market as a result.

The serious day-trader will review daily charts and draw inter-day conclusions about the four key stock index futures markets before beginning the day's trading session.

Tick Charts

The trading system described in this book makes use of tick charts. For the purposes of drawing price bars (OHLC) based on ticks, a tick is considered to be a unique trade of one or more contracts. The price bar interval is then a number of ticks, or trades, completed. For example, a 764-tick chart will draw price bars covering 764 unique trades. The 764-tick bar chart may have any number of contracts traded per bar, but there will be a total of 764 unique trades completed before the next bar is drawn.

Tick charts are popular because they generate price bars based on market activity. When more trades are occurring there are more bars drawn. Some traders find the time distortion created by tick bars to be unacceptable and want price bars that cover a fixed amount of time. For example, in order to gauge the length of a consolidation they do not want time compressed with fewer tick-based bars.

But tick charts allow the user to "see inside" fixed time bars, and often technical indicators will be more responsive with tick-based bars.

The next chart, below, from March 31st, 2010, is an ES 10-minute bar chart. A double bottom price pattern, an extremely well-known price pattern for entering long, is discernable in the second and third bars of the session, but the ten minute fixed interval bars make a trade entry decision difficult.

Immediately following is an ES 764-tick chart from the same date and time. A "reverse head-and-shoulders" (RHS) pattern, another well-known price pattern for entering long, forms and trade entry areas immediately following the first sign of a completed right-hand shoulder are visible. In addition, the tick chart technical indicators show an almost two standard deviation oversold MACD turning up across the head and right shoulder, and a greater than two standard deviation APR price extension. These technical tools help guide the trader.

Of course, the trader will also need to ignore some of the extra activity, or noise, that tick charts generate. Trade setups that are developed with multiple market views help with this, as will be seen later.

E-mini tick charts based on 233-tick intervals, a Fibonacci number[13], have been popular among day-traders[14]. In the past, they gave good bar-by-bar granularity on intra-day charts. But when the CME unbundled its data feed in the Fall of 2009, the 233 setting caused many more tick bars, and traders looked for a larger tick interval that would re-create their previous charts (refer to the Preface).

In the case of the ES contract, 233-tick charts needed to be decreased in their frequency two to three times to give earlier performance. After experimenting with various tick values, the following settings are currently used by the trading system in this book[15]:

TF: 233	NQ: 382
ES: 764	YM: 233

The ES 764-tick chart gives comparable performance to the previous 233-tick chart. The NQ e-mini, which is the second most actively traded e-mini stock index futures contract, appears to coincide with the ES chart with double the tick frequency, or 382 ticks per bar. The TF and YM contracts continue to give good results at the earlier 233-tick setting.

These settings are arbitrary. Users of tick charts will want to experiment with specific intervals until they believe they are seeing enough price action while not creating charts with so many bars that they become a distraction. The 764, 382 and 233 settings may have to change in the future as the e-mini market evolves.

---

[13] 233 is the 13th Fibonacci number (F_{13}). Traders have a fondness for the Fibonacci numbers because of their occurrence in certain descriptions of natural growth phenomenon (perhaps the markets rise and fall similarly?), and not from any demonstrable analysis. The golden ratio $\varphi = (\sqrt{5}+1)/2 \approx 1.618$; $1/\varphi \approx 0.618$; $1 - 0.618 = 0.382 \approx 1/\varphi^2$; $0.618 - 0.382 = 0.236 \approx 1/\varphi^3$; and $1 - 0.236 = 0.764$. If F_n is the nth Fibonacci number, then as n goes to infinity (gets very large), the ratio $F_{n+1} / F_n = \varphi$.
[14] See Mastering the Trade, John Carter, McGraw-Hill, 2006.
[15] There continue to be some examples from the 1st Edition based on ES and NQ 233-tick charts.

March 31, 2010. Where to enter? ES 10-min

March 31, 2010. Reverse H-and-S Pattern. ES 764-tick

Multi-Frame Charting

It is common for traders to look across multiple time-frame charts and the system described here is no exception. Trade setups are more convincing when signals are generated from multiple views of the market. The most common technique is to view charts across multiple time-frames; e.g., 3-minute; 15-minute; 60-minute; Daily.

So that price action is not fixed to static time periods, it can be helpful to trade with tick- and volume-based bar charts. The tick bar chart will draw a new bar after an asset has traded through a number of up- and down-ticks, completing the specified number of trades defined by the tick chart interval size. The volume bar chart will draw a new bar after an asset has traded a fixed number of contracts (or shares). As described already in some detail, the trading system uses tick charts.

The specific charts that are always in use are summarized here. These charts are held on separate displays, or within separate windows on larger multi-window displays, so that they are always viewable without requiring a manual selection.

Market Profile Chart. Because the ES contract is the most studied contract, inter-day price levels and gaps, and Value Areas, are reviewed using a Market Profile chart. Occasionally, a 4-Plex Market Profile view (ES, TF, NQ, YM) is used to study inter-market divergences based on Value Area.

4-Plex 3-Minute Charts. Three minute charts of the four e-mini contracts traded are displayed on a single screen with price levels. This screen is used to review inter-market divergence setups. Individual e-mini screens can be maximized to review individual price level values. 3-Minute charts are often used to set trades.

4-Plex Tick Charts. Tick charts are used to set many of the trades. A 4-plex, single screen view is the default, but when a trade is executed, the e-mini chart in question will be maximized. Statistical MACD (12, 26, 9) and thirty minute APR indicators are applied with overbought/oversold levels defined to be at two standard deviations (2-sigma). A 20-EMA is used for local retracement levels and a custom double-top/double-bottom graphic tool is also applied. The Invivo.Stops trailing stops indicator is applied; see the Trade Management chapter. More will be said about how these indicators are used in the Trade Setups and Trade Management chapters.

CTs 1-Minute Chart. The Cumulative Ticks (CTs) chart based on the NYSE Ticks, as previously described.

A key principle of the e-mini stock index futures trading system described in this book is that a reliance on a single indicator is insufficient to be successful. In other words, there is no trading Holy Grail. Rather, it is a combination of market views and technical indicators which make a viable trading system. Many examples of this style of trading will be given in the Trade Setups chapter.

§§§

Market Price Action

An open market provides an orderly and transparent means of exchanging an asset between Buyers and Sellers. Buyers expect the price of an asset to rise. Sellers expect the price of an asset to fall. Buyers will place bids (referred to as Bids) in the market at a price and quantity that they wish to purchase the asset. Sellers will place offers (referred to as Asks) in the market at a price and quantity that they wish to sell the asset. When the Bid and Ask prices match, a trade will occur, up to the quantity of matching Bids and Asks. The last price at which a trade occurs is said to be the current market price and often referred to simply as "the market."

There can never be more buying than selling, and vice versa. Every transaction consists of an equal amount of buying and selling. The number of unique buying and selling agents, those actually placing orders, may differ, but the total quantity of the asset sold will equal the total quantity of the asset bought. It is at the exchange that disparate buying and selling agents are matched. The exchange matches buying and selling orders, based on Bid-Ask prices and quantities, independent of the trading agents that have placed Bids and Asks. This is the fundamental role of the exchange.

A Buyer may join the market at the Ask, which means to purchase the asset at the current Ask price. A Seller may join the market at the Bid, which means to sell the asset at the current Bid price. Orders where a Buyer joins at the Ask or a Seller joins at the Bid are called Market Orders – the Buyer or Seller complete a trade at what the current market will bear.

Bids and Asks placed ahead of the market (below the market in the case of Bids, above the market in the case of Asks) are referred to as resting orders, and unless they have a price that joins the market, they remain passive orders that do not cause trades to occur. Bids and Asks that join at the market are orders which will cause trades to occur and for this reason are sometimes referred to as active orders[16].

---

[16] See www.marketdelta.com for unique trading software that quantifies the active-passive order dynamic in the market, with unique displays of the Bid and Ask queues. The Market Delta techniques allow the trader to "look inside" price bars.

Below is the NinjaTrader price ladder for the March 2009 ES contract. NinjaTrader is a state-of-the-art PC application that automates order entry and trade strategy execution. The features it offers are an integral part of the e-mini stock index futures system, and more will be said about its use in the chapter Trade Management.

The center highlighted price is the last price (786.75). A parenthesized value next to the price gives the last quantity traded at that price (1). Five Bid quantities with prices at or below the market are shown in the left-hand column. For example, there are 53 ES contracts Bid at 786.25; 58 at 786.00; etc. Five Ask quantities with prices at or above the market are shown in the right-hand column.

These columns, which represent the Bid-Ask queues in the exchange electronic order book, are referred to as Market Depth by the CME and made public. Because NinjaTrader displays the Market Depth data, the price ladder display is commonly referred to as "SuperDOM" (DOM – Depth of Market). While the human trader will find it difficult to make use of this data directly[17], one can imagine software written to use, and provide trade signals from, Market Depth data.

From the price ladder it is clear that unmatched Bids and Asks will neither complete a trade nor move the market (cause a change in current price). Bid prices must move up to Ask prices or Ask prices must move down to Bid prices in order for a trade to occur. When a market participant enters an order at the market this is in fact what will occur. An example helps illustrate this using the price ladder.

Assume a Buyer, trading aggressively, enters an order to Buy 300 ES contracts at the market. The electronic exchange will complete a transaction for 35 contracts at 786.75, because that is the current lowest Ask price and current quantity at that price in the exchange's electronic order book. 35 of the total 300 contracts have traded. Note that if tick charts are being used, then the 35 contracts represent a one tick advance in the tick count of the current bar, even as 35 contracts were traded.

The market is now at 786.75 because that was the last price at which a trade completed. The electronic exchange is aware that a Buy 265 ES

---

[17] Previous generations of "tape readers," traders who acquired the ability to trade from just a stream of continuous market prices (no charts!), may claim that with Market Depth they are able to very successfully scalp the market.

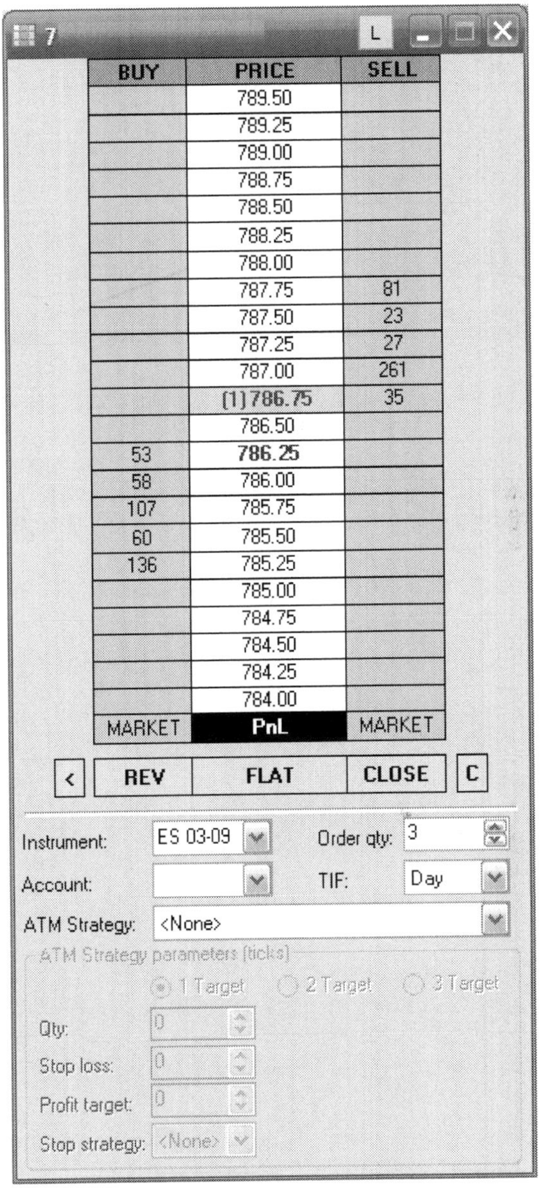

BUY	PRICE	SELL
	789.50	
	789.25	
	789.00	
	788.75	
	788.50	
	788.25	
	788.00	
	787.75	81
	787.50	23
	787.25	27
	787.00	261
	(1) 786.75	35
	786.50	
53	786.25	
58	786.00	
107	785.75	
60	785.50	
136	785.25	
	785.00	
	784.75	
	784.50	
	784.25	
	784.00	
MARKET	PnL	MARKET

| < | REV | FLAT | CLOSE | C |

Instrument: ES 03-09	Order qty: 3
Account:	TIF: Day
ATM Strategy: <None>	

ATM Strategy parameters (ticks)

○ 1 Target ○ 2 Target ○ 3 Target

Qty: 0
Stop loss: 0
Profit target: 0
Stop strategy: <None>

NinjaTrader Price Ladder

contracts at the market remains outstanding and it looks back to the electronic order book and its Ask queue for the next price and quantity available. It finds 261 contracts with an Ask price of 787.00. The exchange will complete a transaction for 261 contracts at 787.00. The market is now at 787.00 and the exchange continues to have an order to Buy 4 (=300-35-261) ES contracts at the market. Once again the exchange moves up its order book to the next Ask price and four more contracts are filled for the Buyer at 787.25. The market is now at 787.25 and the original purchase of 300 contracts is complete.

From the trader's perspective, he or she has completed an order with an average price of [(786.75 x 35) + (787.00 x 261) + (787.25 x 4)] / 300 = 786.9742. From the exchange's perspective the current market has moved to 787.25, with new Market Depth entries indicating the current supply-demand state of the auction. Obviously this entire process is complicated by the real-time introduction of additional Bids, Asks and Market orders. Debugging the electronic exchange's software so that it executes consistently while maintaining a constantly changing electronic order book is no mean feat and the responsibility of the modern, electronic exchange.

The trade example illustrates the following important points:

- Unmatched Bids and Asks do not move market price.
- Bids and Asks with a matching price and Market orders are what move market price because these orders trade, and in so doing they consume Bid-Ask order book entries.
- The market will move based on the aggressiveness of buyers and sellers to either modify their Bid and Ask prices or make use of Market orders.

We conclude from this that a mass mentality that generates a large number of market orders is what rapidly moves price. This fact will be helpful in developing a trading system which seeks to enter the market at well-defined price levels using fixed Bid and Ask prices, referred to as Limit orders, or takes advantage of the way traders use Market orders at key price levels.

Order Entry

There are two important order entry types that are used by the trading system:

- Buy and Sell Limit Orders
- Buy and Sell Stop Market Orders

Buy and Sell Limit Orders are orders with fixed Bid (Buy) and Ask (Sell) prices and quantities.

For example, the order
Buy 2 ESH09 at 786.75 Limit

enters an order to Buy 2 March 2009 ES contracts with a Bid price of 786.75 into the exchange order book. The exchange will complete the order (referred to as "a fill" or simply "filled") at this price (or lower) or fail to do so. A limit order that does not fill is said to "go unable" – an Ask order was not found to match our Bid.

The order
Sell 2 ESH09 at 786.75 Limit

enters an order to Sell 2 March 2009 ES contracts with an Ask price of 786.75 into the exchange order book. The exchange will complete the sale at the specified price (or higher) or go unable – a Bid order was not found to match our Ask.

The trading system uses Limit orders to enter the market, to take profits, and to scratch trades (exit a trade prematurely for no or little loss).

The second order type used is the Stop Market order. This order type is also used to enter the market and plays a critical role in protecting the trader if the market moves against his or her position.

The order
Buy 2 ESH09 at 786.75 Stop

instructs the exchange to Buy 2 March 2009 ES contracts at the Market if the Ask price goes to 786.75.

The order

Sell 2 ESH09 at 786.75 Stop

instructs the exchange to Sell 2 March 2009 ES contracts at the Market if the Bid price goes to 786.75.

Software, will monitor the market and If the Bid or Ask price moves to the Stop Market order price, then an order is issued to join the market at the Bid or Ask; that is, a Market order is sent to the exchange. Because of this there can be execution "slippage": The order may complete one or more ticks from the Stop price in a fast moving market. Because of the enormous liquidity of the e-minis this is typically not an issue.

When Stop Market orders are placed ahead of the market (Buy Stop price above; Sell Stop price below), then the trader executing a trade with forethought. This is different than chasing with Market orders, which is to be avoided. In addition, Stop Market orders are always used to protect trades which go against an opening entry price and to implement "trailing stops" – trailing a winning trade with a succession of price increasing (when Long) or price decreasing (when Short) Stop Market orders so that a trade is closed automatically and profitably.

Stop Market orders are notorious for being a kind of double-edged sword that seemingly cannot be avoided. On the one hand, they have to be used to protect failed trades; on the other, because they are so widely used, they create volume that can prematurely "stop-out" the trader.

Referring to the March 15th, NQ e-mini chart, below, one can imagine a large number of Sell Stop Market orders at the 1903 level, as traders who entered long will have an obvious price level just below their entry which, if breached, is viewed as a significant price level failure that cannot be tolerated. In fact, when well-defined price ledges occur (a buying ledge in this case), they can make for low-risk entries where tight stop-loss Stop Market orders can be placed just outside (above/below) the ledge.

But trading can be doubly frustrating when there is the sense that some larger force is at work testing key price levels in order to shake out the protective Stop Market orders used by the "weak hands." An example of this type of price action is shown in the ES chart from February 12th. While it's demoralizing to experience being stopped out in this fashion, a disciplined use of stop-loss Stop Market orders is advocated by all e-mini

March 15, 2010. Buying Ledge. Sell Stops Below. NQ 3-min

February 12, 2010. Taking out Sell Stops Below? ES 764-tick

day-traders. The only means of avoiding this type of adverse price action is to place stops further outside the ledge or wait for a well-defined price pattern to develop before entering. Here one might have waited for a reverse head-and-shoulders pattern to have formed. More will be said about using price patterns in conjunction with price levels.

A note about the implementation of Limit and Stop Market orders is needed. Limit orders are sent to the exchange order book by the user's desktop trading software. Stop Market orders may be held by the user's desktop trading software or with his broker's network until the Stop price is observed, at which time a Market order is transmitted. In the case of Stop Market orders, the user should be aware of where the market is monitored and the Market order is sent. Local connectivity or PC failures can effect order execution if Stop Market orders are held locally. (A hot-line telephone number to the broker's "trade emergencies" desk is prominently displayed near the trader's desktop, in the event of network or PC failures.)

To address the issue of Stop Market order reliability, a third class of order, the StopLimit order, can be relevant to the e-mini trader. The StopLimit order takes two prices: The Stop price (first price) at which a Limit order, with the second price, is to be entered. Note that in extremely fast markets, if the Limit price is too close to the Stop price, then it is possible that the StopLimit order does not fill. For the e-mini trader, there is an advantage to the StopLimit order as an implementation of stop-loss, because the electronic exchange may accept the StopLimit order and be responsible for its execution. The CME will hold StopLimit orders on its servers. For this reason, NinjaTrader implements Stop Market orders with StopLimit orders. NinjaTrader automatically sets the Limit price to a value that very rarely, if ever, will be exceeded. In the case of the ES contract, NinjaTrader sets the Limit price to be five (5) points above/below the Stop price. The five point value is configurable by the user.

The next NinjaTrader price ladder diagram shows the use of both Limit and Stop Market orders. We have an open order – a Short 2 ESH09 contracts from an entry price of 786.75. The current price is 787.00. A Buy 2 ESH09 788.25 StopLimit (above) is open (Stop price of 788.25; Limit price of 788.25 + 5.00 = 793.25) and protects the short entry from an adverse move in the market. A Buy 1 ESH09 785.25 Limit (below) is open which will take a six tick profit if successful. At that time the two contract stop order will be automatically decreased to one contract by NinjaTrader, and the user can move the stop closer to the market if he or she chooses. The second contract is left open following a profit from the first contract with a winning runner as its goal.

	BUY	PRICE	SELL
		789.50	
		789.25	
		789.00	
		788.75	
		788.50	
2s		788.25	252
		788.00	142
		787.75	104
		787.50	56
		787.25	17
	107	(1) 787.00	
	25	786.75	
	25	786.50	
	88	786.25	
	69	786.00	
		785.75	
		785.50	
1		785.25	
		785.00	
		784.75	
		784.50	
		784.25	
		784.00	
	MARKET	-0.25	MARKET

NinjaTrader Open Position[18]

---

[18] The NinjaTrader graphic shows the software in Simulation Mode. Here the electronic order book is mirrored, or simulated, and the trader can practice without placing real account dollars at risk. Simulator access has become a common day-trading desktop software feature. The NinjaTrader price ladder is shaded when in simulation mode and lightly colored when trading live. Both cases are illustrated in the NinjaTrader examples in this book.

Market Depth Dynamics

When one watches the e-mini markets trade on a regular basis, and has access to Market Depth data – the electronic order book Bid-Ask queues – interesting anomalies can be seen that beg for compelling short-term trade strategies. One can imagine software automation being applied in some of these cases (see the earlier MarketDelta note).

The NinjaTrader SuperDOM from April 8th, 9:11am (Pacific), following the next price chart, below, shows one such example. In the Ask queue we see a relatively large number of resting Sell Limit orders at the 1178.75 – 1179.25 level. At 1179.00 there are over 8000 queued orders, while on the Bid side (left column) the order sizes are in the 2000 – 3000 range. This represents a clear divergence between the Bid-Ask interest at the 1179 price level. Looking at the price chart answers why there might be such a divergence[19].

The next chart is an ES 3-minute price chart from the same date and time. We note that the 1179 price represents opening gap closure. An interpretation of the SuperDOM data is that large numbers of traders are set to fade the closure of the opening gap. This is a well-known and high probability trade, and it has not escaped ES traders during the session. (The large number of limit orders at the 1179 level may also indicate interest to get short ahead of the 1180 price, which may be a short-term BN.)

Based on the SuperDOM data at the 1179 level, two trade strategies come to mind:

1. Make direct use of the known interest to sell and fade from that level. Participate by riding the coattails of the large block of sell orders at 1179, perhaps by placing a limit order 1-tick below, at 1178.75 to help ensure a fill.
2. Knowing that there are a large number of sell orders at 1179, if these are consumed by the market, then we might expect a strong move above. Place a Buy Stop Market order just above the resistance, for example at the 1179.25 or 1179.50 price.

---

[19] It is important to note that only resting Limit Orders are visible in the Market Depth. Market orders are not visible from the exchange order book as they are held on external servers. It would be a great advantage to have access to all the Stop Market orders that have been set. Their existence must be inferred by the trader using price level and price action experience.

The active trader could use both approaches, with tight stop loss in the short case, should price rise quickly through the 1179 level.

Referring again to the ES three minute price chart, we see that gap closure has occurred above the IB High (IBH). The market is IBH Range Extended (RE), and this is considered very bullish. Later, in the Trade Setups chapter, we will cover trades based on the IB. For now, we simply note that the second case, above, might be the preferred trade, given the IBH RE. Again from the April 8th price chart we see that, while the large amount of short interest at 1179 held back the market briefly, the over-riding bullishness of the stock market trumped any futures trading activity and the ES lifted above the 1179 level at approximately 9:30am (Pacific), some 30 minutes after first testing the level.

This example illustrates how the dynamics of Market Depth data can be used when actively day-trading the e-minis.

April 8, 2010. 9:11am Pacific circled. ES 3-min

BUY	PRICE	SELL
	1180.75	
	1180.50	
	1180.25	
	1180.00	
	1179.75	
	1179.50	
	1179.25	7304
	1179.00	8113
	1178.75	5002
	1178.50	3072
	1178.25	827
807	(2)1178.00	
2671	1177.75	
3213	1177.50	
2615	1177.25	
2538	1177.00	
	1176.75	
	1176.50	
	1176.25	
	1176.00	
	1175.75	
	1175.50	
	1175.25	
MARKET	PnL	MARKET

| < | REV | FLAT | CLOSE | C |

Instrument: ES 06-10 ⌄   Order qty: 1 ⇅
Account: ⌄   TIF: Day ⌄
ATM Strategy: <None> ⌄

ATM Strategy parameters (ticks)
◉ 1 Target   ○ 2 Target   ○ 3 Target
Qty: 0 ⇅
Stop loss: 0 ⇅
Profit target: 0 ⇅
Stop strategy: <None> ⌄

April 8, 2010; 9:11 (Pacific) NinjaTrader SuperDOM

Opening Gaps

Many professional traders advocate trading opening gaps – days when the market gaps up or down at the open from the previous day's close. Of course, given the 24 hour nature of electronic Globex trading, there aren't significant gaps in trading the ES, over-night or otherwise. However, from the point of view of the day session, over-night activity can create inter-day gaps, similar to what individual stocks, mostly restricted to day session trading, might exhibit.

My experience with opening gap e-mini trades has been mixed: Some very good winners but also failed trades that have left me demoralized for the rest of the day. Because trade psychology is so important, a trading system that begins with a significant loser right at the start of the day is problematic.

Aware of the adage, "Amateurs open the market and professionals close it," I have tried to bring some data to the issue of trading the day's opening gap.

We begin with a simple opening gap strategy. Its parameters are:

- An opening gap trade is made if the day's open is *N* number of points above or below the previous day's close. *N* is a strategy input parameter that can be optimized. A position is taken after the first minute of the session.
- Stop loss is four ES points (moderate).
- Trailing stop logic that is initiated when the trade is profitable by an amount of 0.75% of contract net value (aggressive) and closes when 50% of total profits are retraced (generous).
- Any open positions are closed at the end of the day's stock market session (4:00pm Eastern).

The next figure is a five year equity curve from the simple automated opening gap strategy (1 ES contract). An example trade (a profitable one) from the automation back-test is also shown.

The equity curve from the opening gap strategy illustrates some of the inherent difficulties in automated trading: Periods of profitability intermixed with long periods of mixed results. It must be said this strategy never lost money, but one wonders how many practitioners could run the program over the first 600 trades, a 30 month duration, with mediocre results?

An optimization of the gap size, *N*, is of interest. Here we generate a curious result. As the table below shows, the strategy was optimal, and by a large margin, with a zero or one point gap-size. This begs the question as to whether we really have an opening gap strategy at all or simply a lucky result from the last two years based on a large number of trades and stop-loss and trailing stop parameters.

The developer's obvious next step is to look for filters that can improve the results of the initial opening gap strategy. While optimizing gap size gave an unconvincing result, using the Market Profile Value Area (VA) is, nonetheless, another approach.

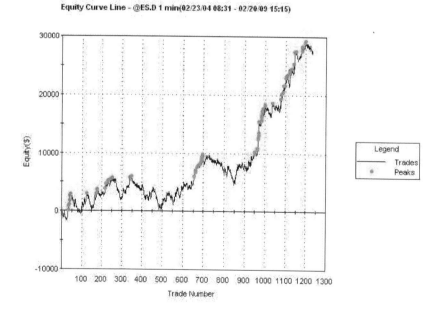

Simple Opening Gap Equity Curve (2/04-2/09). One ES contract

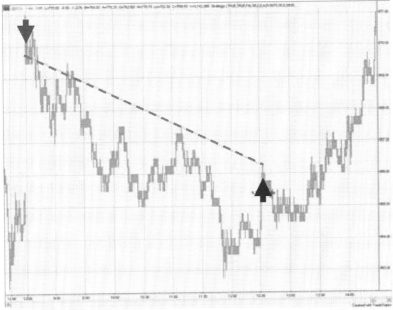

December 26, 2008. Opening Gap Strategy Example. ES 1-min

The idea is to require the gap to be outside (above or below) the previous day's VA. This idea represents one of the many ways Market Profile information can be traded. The next chart shows a Market Profile distribution with an opening gap below the previous day's value area. If gaps take the market outside the previous day's VA, isn't this a sign of price extension with reversion back to the VA likely? (Of course, one can argue whether the trader should have been considering any long positions from a gap down during the extraordinary bear market in which this chart was taken – January 2009; but a back-test over a number of previous years is easily conducted.)

The initial gap strategy was enhanced to use a VA filter and the next chart shows its five year equity curve. Even as the last 150 trades gave spectacular results, it was concluded that the VA filter does not provide a large overall improvement relative to the original version.

The final table gives key performance data for the original Opening Gap strategy (no VA filter). At a high-level its performance is impressive: A 26% annualized return and 314% return on initial account margin over five years ($10,000 for the one e-mini contract traded). However, when we look at the performance summary further we see inherent problems that are difficult for the implementer. Specifically, the trader must endure a 60% losing percentage and up to 11 losing trades in a row.

While one can argue this is simply a part of the larger endeavor of trading, how many of us can tolerate 11 losing trades in a row without throwing in the towel? And when it's a piece of software that is losing money, it becomes difficult to leave the program on-line. I have found that automated strategies need to deliver a 60% winning percentage to be psychologically viable on an on-going basis.

To summarize: Opening gap trades are widely advocated by the day-trading community. An analysis shows that in their simplest form they do not give a large enough winning percentage to be traded with conviction. Additional research is required to find filters that can help with the opening gap trade. Certainly, the data here are not comprehensive and there is much room for investigating additional filters.

While it is true that the opening gap trade relies on good price level structure (the gap) and can be hugely profitable, it is also the case that beginning the trading day with a loser is psychologically difficult. As such, opening gaps are not one of the trade setups advocated in the Trade Setups chapter. There we will see how additional information improves the winning percentage of the trading system and meets the criteria of developing a system that uses a variety of signals in order to trade.

Opening Gap Closure

Even as opening gap trades are currently not defined, opening gap *closure* trades do appear to be a high probability trade. When gap closure occurs and other factors do not mitigate against it (e.g., Unequivocal CTs that indicate a trend), the trader can be on the lookout for fading opening gap closure.

Back-testing a simple gap closure strategy gives promising results. Using similar stop loss and trailing stop parameters as in the opening gap tests, and a minimum gap size of 12 points, a very positive equity curve is generated from a five year back-test. While opening gaps of 12 points or more are rare, when back-testing produces the type of equity curve shown here, and with an 83% profitable trade percentage, it is something that deserves a trader's attention.

OpenGapValue	Net Profit	% Profitable
0	27755	41
1	22843	40
6	15593	42
8	15383	43
2	15198	39
7	15008	42
3	14955	39
4	14508	40
5	13813	41
10	11555	44
9	10383	42
11	9450	43
13	8130	43
12	8128	43
14	7603	45
15	6218	45
20	4658	47
17	4490	44
16	4418	44
18	4393	45
19	4203	45

Opening Gap Strategy: Optimal Gap Size

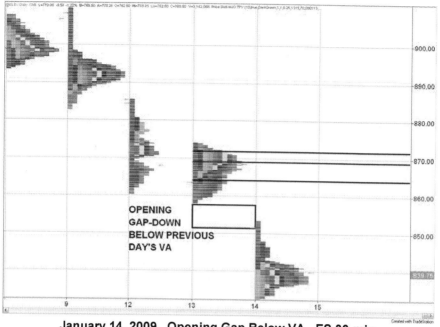

January 14, 2009. Opening Gap Below VA. ES 30-min

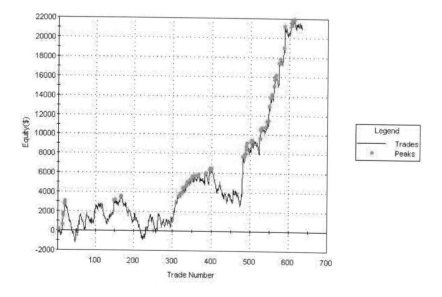

Opening Gap Strategy with VA Filter (2/04-2/09). One ES contract

TradeStation Performance Summary

	All Trades	Long Trades	Short Trades
Total Net Profit	$27,755.00	$16,725.00	$11,030.00
Gross Profit	$170,102.50	$82,375.00	$87,727.50
Gross Loss	($142,347.50)	($65,650.00)	($76,697.50)
Profit Factor	1.19	1.25	1.14
Total Number of Trades	1234	595	639
Percent Profitable	40.68%	43.70%	37.87%
Winning Trades	502	260	242
Losing Trades	732	335	397
Even Trades	0	0	0
Max. Consecutive Winning Trades	7	7	5
Max. Consecutive Losing Trades	11	7	10
Max. Shares/Contracts Held	1	1	1
Annual Rate of Return	26.60%		
Max. Equity Run-up	$31,440.00		
Date of Max. Equity Run-up	12/29/08		
Max. Equity Run-up as % of Initial Capital	314.40%		
Max. Drawdown (Intra-day Peak to Valley)			
Value	($6,122.50)	($3,515.00)	($6,822.50)
Date	03/02/06		
as % of Initial Capital	61.23%	35.15%	68.22%
Max. Trade Drawdown	($375.00)	($262.50)	($375.00)

Opening Gap Strategy Performance. One ES contract

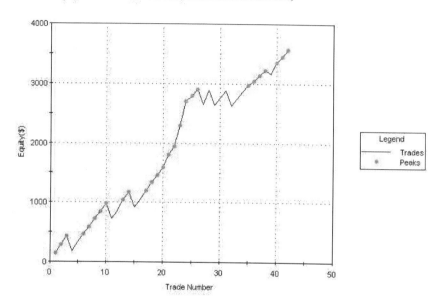

Rudimentary Opening Gap Closure Strategy (5/05-5/10). One ES contract

Price Patterns

The trader who follows a market regularly will, over time, discern patterns in his or her charts that appear to lead to profitable trades.

Trading based on pattern matching is certainly not an exact science:

- Patterns do not repeat identically. Given the vagaries of discretionary trading, a pattern that appears valid one moment may not give the trader the same confidence when encountered later under slightly different conditions.
- Most traders have not quantified the success rate of trades based on well-defined patterns, and so it is difficult to say, objectively, whether trading a pattern is valid[1].

And yet, trading with perceived price patterns is an active and long-standing craft among technical traders. The numerous candlestick chart variations and their quaint names (e.g., long legged and dragonfly dojis), the tried and true double tops and double bottoms, perhaps part of every trader's arsenal, the purportedly ultra-reliable head and shoulders, and ascending and descending triangles and wedges, are just a few of the well-known, and much discussed and utilized patterns referenced by active traders.

If nothing else, price patterns help the user navigate the ubiquitous noise and the inherent uncertainty at the right edge of the price chart. Because price patterns bring some form to a chart they are compelling, even as the market's unfolding price action is ultimately unknowable.

When a price pattern can be given a convincing rationale, then it is hard to ignore. It may be that the patterns are not any more or less effective than any other entry decision technique, and the true value of a perceived price pattern is that it evokes a roughly equivalent response from the trader. In other words, price patterns discipline the trader to a

---

[1] See the text Evidence-Based Technical Analysis, David R. Aronson, John Wiley & Sons, 2007. Aronson makes a compelling case that traders fool themselves into seeing chart patterns which have not been quantified.

regular repetition of performance, and even if flawed, that repetition gives better results than those that are more random.

Take, for example, perhaps the best known price pattern – the double bottom. The double bottom price pattern is shown both schematically and with a candlestick chart, below.

The interpretation of the double bottom is that the market first tests, or discovers, a new lower price level. This occurs at (1) in the schematic, the first bottom. After some speculative buying (those seeking to trade a possible reversal at the most profitable point) and short-side covering (those who were short and are satisfied with profits at the new lower level), the market re-tests the newly discovered low at (2) in the schematic. There are three outcomes to the re-test at (2):

1. The market consolidates at this level, perhaps for a relatively lengthy period of time.
2. The market sells off further, through this level, and makes new lows.
3. The price level holds and the market now reverses. The strength of the reversal initially is unknown.

It is an easy matter to review a new long position from this simple analysis:

1. A long from (1) is aggressive trading. A trader taking a position from (1) does so with relatively little information as it is by definition new territory for the market.
2. A long following the retest at (2) is making use of significant additional information; namely, the previous low (1) has held and it may be the case that the market will now reverse or at least consolidate.

From this type of analysis and interpretation of price action, the experienced trader will look for a double bottom against which to trade. He or she is buying low while taking advantage of evidence of support based on a successful re-test (2) of the previous low (1).

Double Bottom Price Pattern: Schematic and Candlestick Bars

The 1st Edition of this book referenced double tops and bottoms and third time patterns. Price patterns are compelling when a plausible rationale motivating their use is available, as in the case of the double bottom. The use of price patterns makes trade entry decisions more precise.

Here are a small set of price patterns that the e-mini trading system now incorporates on a regular basis.

We organized market price action based on the following four principles:

- Day-Type
- Price Levels
- Technical Indication (of price extension and retracement)
- Time-of-Day Patterns

Now a fifth component is added: Price Pattern. Specific price patterns are included in the analysis to give trade setups greater definition. They serve to augment the other four market views and improve the trading.

Because there are hundreds of price patterns to choose from[2], the reader will undoubtedly ask, How is it that you've sufficiently covered the area or, perhaps even worse, added too many patterns, so that the trading becomes overly complicated?   The patterns documented here are relatively straightforward, have been derived after watching the market

---

[2] There are a number of books dedicated to a review of chart patterns. See for example, Encyclopedia of Chart Patterns, Thomas N. Bulkowski, Wiley Trading, 2005, and Trade Chart Patterns Like the Pros, Suri Duddella, 2008.

daily for a number of years, include trend, breakout and reversal trades, cover both long and short entries fairly equally, and are considered to be the best of the lot. The number of patterns has been kept small so as to not overly complicate the trading.

This chapter covers the patterns and the Trade Setups chapter puts them to use.

The price patterns are organized by direction, Long or Short, and category: Trend, Breakout and Reversal.

Each price pattern is described with the following information:

- A schematic of the pattern showing the trade entry opportunities offered by the pattern.
- Categorization of the pattern as Trend, Breakout or Reversal.
- A rationale as to why the price pattern is used.
- Trade entry options.
- Additional notes to help qualify the pattern.
- A trade on a price chart that illustrates the pattern in practice.

A table at the end of the chapter summarizes the price patterns for quick reference.

EMA SHORT

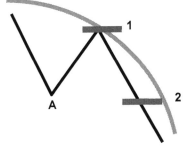

Classification: Trend. One of the most well-known trend-following technical patterns.

Rationale: The EMA offers a local retracement level against which to trade. If the market is trending, an EMA retracement entry defines a means of getting on the trend without chasing. An initial stop-loss level is well-defined, just outside the EMA line.

Entry:
- Sell Limit order at the 20-EMA line.
- Sell Stop Market order 1-2 ticks below the previous minimum (A).

Notes:
- 20-EMA' < 0 (rate of change of the EMA is negative).
- If a Limit order is used (Entry 1), then a low-risk initial stop-loss several ticks above the EMA can be used.

A general note about the differences between Entry 1 and 2 is in order. Entry 1 can make use of a tighter initial stop-loss, just above the EMA line in the case of the EMA SHORT. Entry 2 probably requires a wider initial stop-loss. Some traders prefer the Stop Market order, Entry 2, as it opens a position only when the market is moving in the direction of the trade. See the Trade Management chapter for a quantitative assessment of the Entry 1/2 difference.

These entry guidelines will apply to the other Entry 1 and 2 cases across the price patterns, and in both long and short cases.

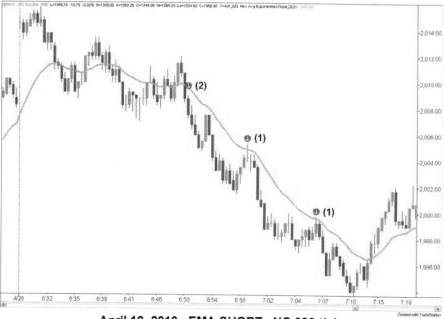

April 10, 2010. EMA SHORT. NQ 382-tick

MML SHORT (Momentum Move with Ledge)

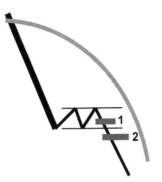

Classification: Trend

Rationale: A new trend following a reversal is indicated by a strong momentum move in price. A short-term ledge forms as the market briefly consolidates before continuing in the direction of the trend. The ledge offers an opportunity to get on the trend without chasing.

Entry:
- Sell Limit, near the market, at the first signs of a completed ledge top. Aggressive.
- Sell Stop Market 1-2 ticks below supporting ledge. Conservative.

Notes:
- 20-EMA' < 0.
- Tick charts can be used to identify temporary consolidation ledges.
- The trade has a higher probability of success when used after the first recognizable momentum move.

May 4, 2010. MML SHORT. TF 233-tick

3TD SHORT (Third Time Down)

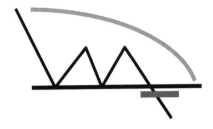

Classification: Breakout

Rationale: The pattern can be considered a double bottom which did not hold. The third time test of a price level often results in a breakout. The Sell Stop order triggers only on the breakout.

Entry:
- Sell Stop Market 1-2-ticks below the support level.

Notes:
- 20-EMA' < 0.
- The higher probability setup has "air" under the support level. That is, the setup can be used at the day's lows, but in that case it has a lower probability of success.
- The 3TD SHORT is an example of a descending triangle pattern, considered one of the more reliable breakout chart patterns in a bear market.

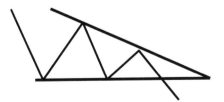

March 26, 2010. 3TD SHORT. YM 233-tick

BOP SHORT (Breakout Pullback)

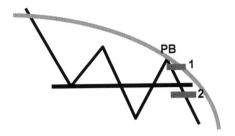

Classification: Breakout

Rationale: An initial breakout of a significant price level indicates the market may continue in the direction of the breakout. A pullback entry offers a low-risk trade that takes advantage of the breakout attempt.

Entry:
- Sell Limit at the first sign of Pullback (PB) completion. The 20-EMA can be used as a price level. Aggressive.
- Sell Stop Market 1-2 ticks below original breakout level following the pullback. Conservative.

Notes:
- 20-EMA' < 0.
- Entry may be very similar to an EMA SHORT, but the trade type is different. The BOP is a breakout trade; the EMA is generally trend-following.
- It is similar to the 3TD SHORT, but has both Limit and Stop Market entries.
- It is similar to the PDT SHORT; see below. However this is a breakout trade and the PDT SHORT is a reversal trade. Also, note the difference in orientation of the 20-EMA in the BOP SHORT and the PDT SHORT.
- When the PB level is equal to the Breakout level, then the trade is the same as a Support Becomes Resistance (SBR) trade.

February 10, 2010. BOP SHORT. ES 764-tick

3TF SHORT (Third Time Failure)

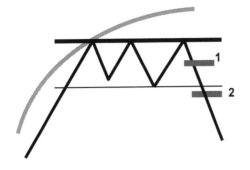

Classification: Reversal. A failed third time up test of a previous maximum can lead to a reversal.

Rationale: The market has failed a third time up test. We generally expect markets to succeed with third time tests and the failure represents a trading opportunity.

Entry:
- Sell Limit at first sign of Third Time Up failure. Aggressive.
- Sell Stop Market below recent support ledge. Conservative.

Notes:
- 20-EMA' → 0. Slope of 20-EMA approaching 0.
- Entry 1 uses a Limit order that is very close to the market. On the first sign of the third time failure, the market is entered.
- When Entry 2 is used, the setup is very similar to the 3TD SHORT, however the trader's perspective is different. The 3TF SHORT is based on resistance level success. The 3TD SHORT is based on a support level failure.
- Topping pattern after an extended move is part of the setup. If the two right-most tops are showing lower highs, then it becomes a higher probability setup.
- Key Price Level makes for a better setup.
- This setup can be considered the short version of the RHS LONG; see below.

February 9, 2010. 3TF SHORT. ES 764-tick

PDT SHORT (Price Double Top)

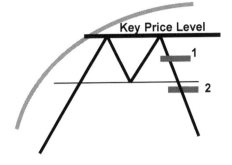

Classification: Reversal

Rationale: The market has failed to break through a key price level on a second attempt. If the price level is significant, then we can expect the market to retrace, at least temporarily. Note: the 3TF trade is often a higher probability trade. The Double Top variation requires a key price level component.

Entry:
- Sell Limit at Price Level minus 1-2 ticks (resting) or at first sign of Double Top formation (close to the market). Aggressive.
- Sell Stop Market below a recent support ledge. Conservative.

Notes:
- 20-EMA' → 0. Slope of 20-EMA approaching 0.
- Entry 1 can use a Limit order that is very close to the market.
- Because the topping pattern is limited to a double-top, a well-defined price level is critical: IBH; PDH; DPH; etc. The setup can be considered a more aggressive version of the 3TF SHORT.
- If the right top is lower than the left, then it can be a higher probability setup.
- Shorting from the first maximum of the Double-Top is aggressive trading.

March 24, 2010. PDT SHORT. ES 764-tick

In this last example, the IB High (IBH) was used as the key price level. The trade was motivated by flat, Equivocal CTs, as shown in the next chart. More will be said about these kinds of corroborating views of the market and the trade setups they generate.

March 24, 2010. ES 1-min

EMA LONG

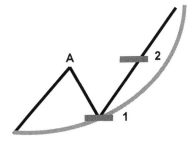

Classification: Trend. One of the most well-known trend-following technical patterns.

Rationale: The EMA offers a local retracement level against which to trade. If the market is trending, an EMA retracement entry defines a means of getting on the trend without chasing. An initial stop-loss level is well-defined, just outside the EMA line.

Entry:
- Buy Limit order at the 20-EMA line.
- Buy Stop Market order 1-2 ticks above the previous local maximum (A).

Notes:
- 20-EMA' > 0 (rate of change of the EMA is positive).
- If a Limit order is used (Entry 1), then a low-risk initial stop-loss several ticks below the entry price can be used.

April 8, 2010. EMA LONG. ES 764-tick

MML LONG (Momentum Move with Ledge)

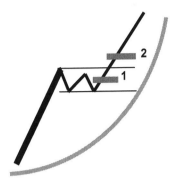

Classification: Trend

Rationale: A new trend following a reversal is indicated by a strong momentum move in price. A short-term ledge forms as the market briefly consolidates before continuing in the direction of the trend. The ledge offers an opportunity to get on the trend without chasing.

Entry:
- Buy Limit, near the market, at the first signs of a completed ledge bottom. Aggressive.
- Buy Stop Market 1-2 ticks above resistance ledge. Conservative.

Notes:
- 20-EMA' > 0.
- Tick charts can be used to identify temporary consolidation ledges.
- The trade has a higher probability of success when used after the first recognizable momentum move of a reversal.

February 11, 2010. MML LONG. ES 764-tick

BOP LONG (Breakout Pullback)

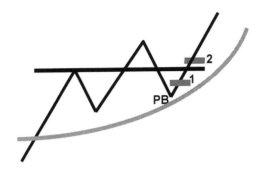

Classification: Breakout

Rationale: An initial breakout of a significant price level indicates the market may continue in the direction of the breakout. A pullback entry offers a low-risk trade that takes advantage of the breakout attempt.

Entry:
- Buy Limit at the first sign of Pullback (PB) completion. The 20-EMA can be used as a price level. Aggressive.
- Buy Stop Market 1-2 ticks above original breakout level. Conservative.

Notes:
- 20-EMA' > 0.
- Entry may be very similar to an EMA LONG, but the trade type is different. The BOP is a breakout trade; the EMA is generally trend-following.
- The trader may have a preference to enter long breakouts after a pullback.
- When the PB level is equal to the Breakout level, then the trade is the same as a Resistance Becomes Support (RBS) trade.

March 25, 2010. BOP LONG. ES 764-tick

3TU LONG (Third Time Up)

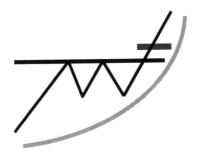

Classification: Breakout

Rationale: The market has succeeded in a third time up test. A successful third time up is a sign of market strength in the direction of the test. Trade entry on the breakout takes advantage of a successful third time up.

Entry:
- Buy Stop Market 1-2 ticks above the resistance level.

Notes:
- 20-EMA' > 0.
- The 3TU LONG is an example of an ascending triangle, considered one of the more reliable breakout chart patterns in a bull market.

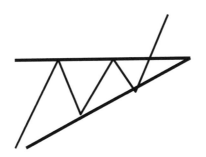

March 12, 2010. 3TU LONG. NQ 382-tick

RHS LONG (Reverse Head and Shoulders)

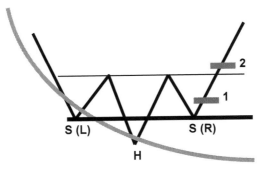

Classification: Reversal

Rationale: The market tests (H) a level of prior support (S(L)) with new price discovery, which seems to be a common phenomenon in futures trading. The market holds on a third test of the general area of support (S(R)), which offers a possible high probability trade entry.

Entry:
- Buy Limit at first sign of right shoulder formation, just above neckline. Aggressive.
- Buy Stop Market 1-2 ticks just above shoulder line. Conservative.

Notes:
- 20-EMA' → 0. Slope of 20-EMA approaching 0. It may also be the case that 20-EMA' > 0. It is critical not to take the trade with 20-EMA' < 0, which is the well-known "catching a falling knife" trade.
- Entry 1 uses a Limit order that is very close to the market. On the first sign of a push-up from the support level, the market is entered.
- The setup may be considered the long version of the 3TF and PTD SHORT.
- A variation to the Reverse Head and Shoulders is the Double-Bottom with Pullback. In this case, the left shoulder and head levels are the same and form a Double-Bottom. This pattern variation is shown below.

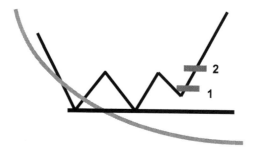

RHS Variant: Double Bottom with Pullback Long

April 16, 2010. RHS LONG. ES 764-tick

Since the introduction to price patterns used the double bottom example as motivation, the reader will want to know, What happened to the double bottom — Why has it not been identified as one of the selected price patterns?

Experience trading the e-mini stock index futures shows that the RHS is a preferred reversal long entry pattern, as the market will often execute price discovery before turning up, which is the head (H) in the RHS pattern. Also, the double bottom with pullback entry is covered by the RHS pattern. Some readers will want to rely on the original double bottom, in any case.

In the RHS Long example, trade entry was just above the ES 1200 price level, with 1200 certainly a very Big Number (BN). Again, an example of coordinating multiple market views, in this case the price pattern with a recognized BN. There will be numerous examples of this in the Trade Setups chapter.

The experienced trader will be able to easily describe his or her trade setups concisely, and it will become second nature to quickly make a statement such as, "The last trade was a 3TU Long from the IB high; CTs remained bullish."

Regardless of the specific trading system used, one expects the serious trader to describe trades with an equivalently detailed nomenclature.

Price Pattern Summary

The Price Patterns can be organized into a short-hand reference table with relationships between the patterns shown to help in their recognition and use.

	Trend	Breakout	Reversal
SHORT	EMA	3TD	3TF
	MML	BOP(SBR)	PDT
LONG	EMA	3TU	RHS*(3TF)
	MML	BOP(RBS)	PDB**

Price Pattern Reference Table

There are a number of correlations among the patterns:

- Inverse Patterns
    EMA SHORT and LONG are inverses
    MML SHORT and LONG
    3TD SHORT and 3TU LONG
    BOP SHORT and BOP LONG
    3TF/PDT SHORT and RHS LONG
- Equivalent Patterns (same structure, slightly different interpretation)
    BOP SHORT and SBR SHORT (Support Becomes Resistance)
    BOP LONG and RBS LONG (Resistance Becomes Support)
- Additional Notes
    * The RHS LONG can be considered a 3TF LONG
    **A PDB LONG (Price Level Double-Bottom Long) pattern is not called out individually but incorporated in a variant of the RHS

Trade Setups

This chapter gives the specific trade setups and signals that make up the e-mini stock index futures day-trading system.

The trade setups are built from five basic market analyses:

- Day-Type
- Price Levels
- Technical Indication
- Time-of-Day Patterns
- Price Pattern[1]

Once in the market, automated stop-loss and profit-targets are used to exit a position. These are covered in the next chapter, Trade Management.

As discussed in the chapter on Trading Basics, the trading system attempts to bring a number of different techniques and perspectives into play in order to identify high probability trades. However, the system must also be straightforward to use and easily repeatable. The price patterns are intended to help in this regard.

Before defining the specific setups which make up the trading system, examples of how the five market analyses are used together to identify high-probability trades are given.

The first is a long entry in the TF e-mini (Russell 2000) from February 25, 2009. The next three charts illustrate the trade setup.

First, Day-Type is classified as not a Trend Day[2] based on an Equivocally bearish CTs reading. Even though the Dow is off over 100 points at the time the trade is made, the CTs are range-bound and do not indicate a Trend Day. This allows a long position if a high-probability price level reversal can be identified.

---

[1] Newly incorporated with the book's 2nd Edition.
[2] Days that are *not* Trend Days include Normal, Neutral, Double Distribution and Non-Trend days.

Second, we notice the TF contract tested the Previous Day's Low (PDL).

Third, an oversold MACD on the TF 233-tick chart indicates we are trading on the right side of the technical indicator. This, along with the fact that the CTs are not indicating a trend, is the technical indication component of the trade.

Fourth, we will enter the trade just before 1:00pm Eastern, a period when afternoon rallies can begin. We make sure not to enter the trade during the noon hour when non-trending congestion could defeat us. If there is an afternoon rally, we will be positioned for it. Time-of-Day has now been factored into the position.

Fifth, we execute the trade using an RHS LONG price pattern.

Finally, automated software, which will be discussed in the Trade Management chapter, is used to set a low-risk stop-loss, take an initial fast profit, and then move stop-loss to break even, in order to get the trade to an on-the-house, no-lose position as soon as possible.

The fourth chart in the series shows how the trade performed 30 minutes after entry.

February 25, 2009. Equivocal CTs

February 25, 2009. TF at the Previous Day's Low. TF 3-min

February 25, 2009. MACD-Price Divergence and RHS LONG. TF 233-tick

February 25, 2009. TF Long Trade. TF 233-tick

The next set of example trades, from May 6, 2010, again illustrates how the various market views are put together by the trader.

The ES daily chart from May 6, 2010 shows the market in a recent bear move after a strong spring-time rally. An intermediate bull trend line beginning in February has been broken. There are fundamental economic factors at play – the Euro debt crisis – as well as technical factors – an overly robust U.S. stock market rally following the 2008/9 crash has many analysts figuring overbought conditions. The VIX volatility index, a measure of SP option pricing, has increased dramatically (16 to 26 in the last 10 sessions, more than a 60% increase).

On May 6th the market opens gap down (6.25 ES points) and the gap is closed within the first 30 minutes of the session but moves no higher. The CTs are flat to down during the first hour of trading; see charts, below. The overall view of the trading day develops:

- Inter-day bearish
- Gap closed and not exceeded
- CTs bearish

and the day-trader looks for short setups.

May 6, 2009. ES Daily

Within the first hour the ES tick chart shows a "Third Time Up" failure. This is the basis for the 3TF SHORT price pattern. The 3TF at the gap closure level makes for a compelling setup. This, or a PDT short from the double top, might have been the first trade of the day. See the ES 764-tick chart, below.

After the first hour, the IB has formed and the focus becomes IB Range Extension or Reversal. An overall short bias does not change when a review of the CTs shows the market continues to sell. Sure enough, after finding short-term support at the IBL, the market moves below the IBL with Range Extension (RE). IBL RE in the context of Unequivocally Bearish CTs adds to the overall bearish focus for the day thus far. The trader looks for a price pattern to enter short.

The aggressive trader may use a Sell Stop Market order at 1-2 ticks below the IBL. An alternative is to view the IBL RE as a breakout and look for retracement to the IBL for a slightly later entry using the BOP SHORT price pattern. This is shown in the next ES 764-tick chart.

May 6, 2009. First Hour – Flat CTs. ES 1-min

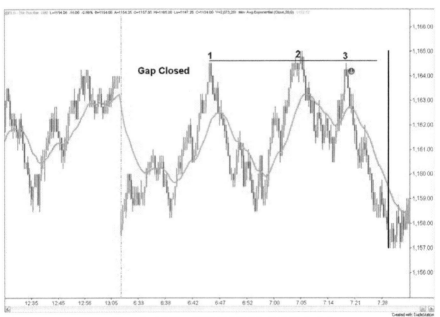

May 6, 2009. 3TF SHORT. ES 764-tick

May 6, 2009. BOP SHORT. ES 764-tick

(The astute trader may have also used a 3TD SHORT and a prior BOP SHORT. These additional short entries are marked on the chart as well.)

In fact, this session[3] offered many good trades, long and short. A successful, and gutsy, long setup occurred near the ES 1150 BN minus two point level.

Recognizing the 1150 BN and the 1148 two point discovery range, an aggressive trader could have made use of the RHS LONG price pattern. (Note: The author did not take this trade.) In the case of the RHS long, the 20-EMA rate-of-change (20-EMA') must move to zero or above. *DO NOT* take an RHS long trade unless the 20-EMA' has at least moved to zero. Two additional EMA LONG entries are shown on the chart, as well.

---

[3] This section was drafted while trading just prior to the historic May 6, 2010 afternoon sell-off that had the Dow losing close to 1000 points before recovering some 600 and closing down 347 points on the day. It was a panic exacerbated by computerized trading and the most violent intra-day sell-off in the history of the NYSE.

May 6, 2009. RHS and EMA LONG. ES 764-tick

May 6, 2009. BOP SHORT on IBL Retracement. ES 3-min

Finally, a three minute ES chart from the session shows a retracement to exactly one tick off the IBL, almost two hours after the IB was formed. This made for another BOP SHORT trade, the pullback occurring over a long duration by day-trading standards. It is remarkable how a market based on such varied activity as the S&P 500 index can perform so predictably with respect to a number of price levels, both absolute – the 1150 BN – and intrinsic, the IBL. (And then the Dow crashed more than 500 points. So much for predictability!).

As with the price pattern descriptions, the trade setups are organized using the standard categories:

- Trend
- Breakout
- Reversal

To which are added two new categories:

- Divergence
- Market Profile[4]

Specific price patterns are identified, and a set of example trades are given, for each of the trade setups

Stop-loss and profit-target guidelines are not detailed in the setup descriptions but are provided in the Trade Management chapter that follows.

A small schematic accompanies the trade setup description for easy identification.

---

[4] Using Market Profile theory to actively day-trade has recently become increasing popular. This section provides additional Market Profile trade setups to address the interest in trading with the Market Profile.

Trend Trades

Trend trades have a high probability of success when the Day-Type is determined to be a Trend Day, although there can be other day types when trends occur during part of the session and trend trading works well.

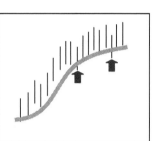

The CTs indicator is used to indicate a Trend Day, and when the CTs are Unequivocal that is one of the best predictors of a Trend Day.

Trend Days are traded with the following price patterns:

- **EMA:** A 20-EMA local retracement on 3-minute or tick charts.

- **MML:** The trader enters after a momentum move using a short-term ledge.

- **BOP:** Price level retracements that occur within a larger trend.

Trend trades following an IB RE can be high probability trades. In addition, there is an afternoon rally phenomenon that is often prevalent in the U.S. stock market and which can make for good trend trades; see the special section, below.

Example(s):

January 2, 2009. A classic trend day. CTs are Unequivocally bullish. IB RE occurs off a narrow IB. Also, the RE quickly moves above the previous day's high (PDH). Because of the bullishness shown by the CTs and the price level extensions, we enter on a local retracement to the 3-minute 20-EMA (EMA LONG).

February 23, 2009. Moderate IB width and CTs are Unequivocally bearish. The market is entered with a resting limit order at the IBL following initial range extension (BOP SHORT).

February 24, 2009. IB RE occurs in the afternoon. CTs move from Equivocal to Unequivocally bullish. Shorts should now be avoided. Once Unequivocally bullish CTs are identified, the trader looks to enter on a 3-minute 20-EMA retracement (EMA LONG).

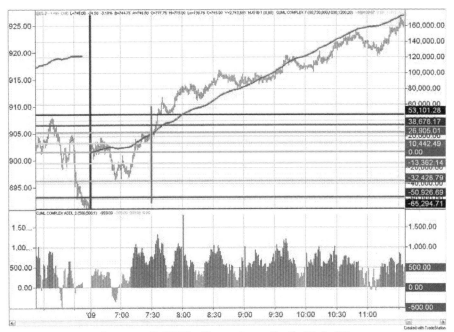

January 2, 2009. Unequivocally Bullish CTs

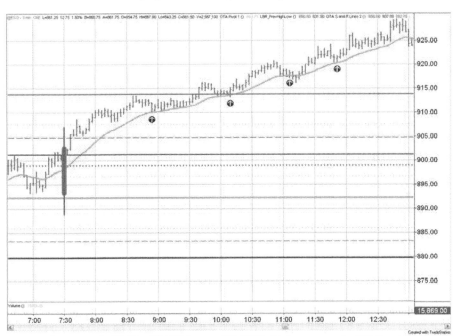

January 2, 2009. IB RE Long, 20-EMA Retracement. ES 3-min

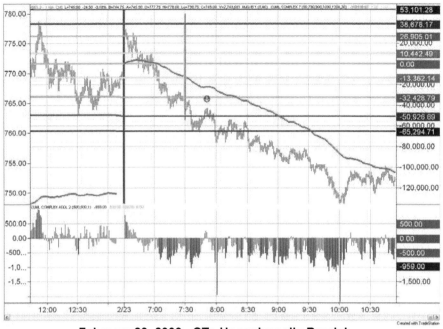

February 23, 2009. CTs Unequivocally Bearish

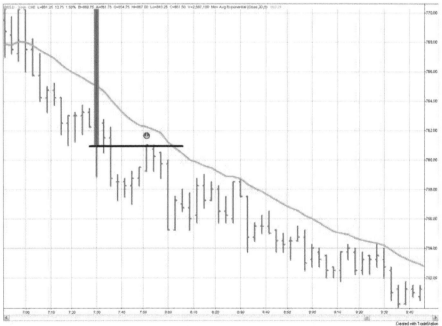

February 23, 2009. IB RE Short at IBL Retracement. ES 3-min

February 24, 2009. CTs Become Unequivocally Bullish

February 24, 2009. Afternoon Rally with IB RE. ES 3-min

February 9, 2010. CTs move from Equivocal to Unequivocally bullish and are indicating a reversal – no negative CTs histogram bars. IB RE occurs just before noon (9am Pacific). The ES 3-minute chart shows a good momentum move, and the ES tick chart has a well-defined ledge that can be used for a low-risk entry; that is, stop-loss can be set just under the ledge (MML LONG). Here is a coincidence of the MML and EMA LONG patterns on the tick chart.

February 23, 2010. Strong momentum move push down in the ES on a 3-minute chart. A ledge offers a low-risk entry. Stop-loss can be set just above the ledge (MML SHORT).

February 9, 2010. CTs Indicate Reversal Rally. ES 1-min

February 9, 2010. Momentum Move and Ledge (MML). ES 3-min

February 9, 2010. MML LONG. ES 764-tick

February 23, 2010. MML SHORT. ES 3-min

Trend Trades: Afternoon Rallies (Special Topic)

Afternoon rallies seem to be a common occurrence in the stock market, even during bear markets. Market watchers consider an afternoon rally to be a sign of bullishness.

The trader uses Time-of-Day along with an Unequivocal bullish CTs indication to enter afternoon rallies. In this regard, watching the market for support during the last half of the noon hour (NYSE) or prior to the afternoon pivot 1:30pm (NYSE) is helpful when entering an afternoon rally.

Trends can be very difficult to trade and many day-traders prefer days that are not Trend days, when price reversals are available to fade. On strong Trend Days, there is the sense that "the train has already left the station and I don't know how to get on."

The e-mini stock index futures trader who prefers to short the market and gets on the wrong side of an afternoon rally will have a difficult time. Some traders claim that the most difficult time to be short is between 1:00pm and 2:00pm (Eastern).

If the trader is tempted to short an afternoon rally which, it must be said, can be difficult to avoid, then he or she should wait until the last hour of the session and carefully study price action to identify rally exhaustion. If CTs become Equivocal, then there may be support for shorting an afternoon rally in the last hour. More is said about afternoon rallies in the Trade Examples chapter.

Afternoon Rally trade entry uses retracement to a 20-EMA on a 3-minute chart or from the bottom of a consolidation buying ledge on either a 3-minute or tick chart. In the latter case, if the initial afternoon rally "lift-off" is missed, a 20-EMA retracement on the tick chart can be used to avoid chasing. The buying ledge offers a low-risk entry position in that stop-loss can be set just below the ledge.

See the January 28, 2009 trade example from the Inter-Market Divergence section of the chapter for a good example of a buying ledge.

Example(s):

December 5, 2008. The day begins with CTs Unequivocally bearish. By the lunch hour the market has flattened. CTs have become Equivocal. At the start of the afternoon session (10:00am Pacific, 1:00pm Eastern) the market begins to show signs of a rally. The aggressive trader may enter near the end of the lunch hour in order to be positioned for a possible afternoon rally. The more conservative trader may wait for further evidence of a rally. An 11:00am (Pacific) IBH RE adds to the conviction that we are seeing an afternoon rally, and a 20-EMA retracement entry coincides with a retracement to the IBH (BOP LONG). There is one more chance to enter on an aggressive retracement to the 3-minute 20-EMA at the beginning of the last hour of the day (EMA LONG).

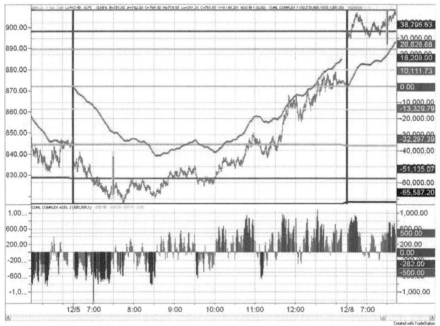

December 5, 2008. CTs Unequivocally Bearish to Bullish

December 5, 2008. Afternoon Rally. ES 3-min

Breakout Trades

Breakout trades can be based on local extrema – localized price levels established during the trading session, or more significant price levels – DPH/L, IBH/L, PDH/L, Pivot, Open, and inter-day support and resistance. Breakout trades that leverage the more significant price levels may make for higher probability of trades.

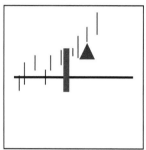

Breakout trades are entered using Stop Market orders or Limit orders. The 3TD (Third Time Down) and 3TU (Third Time Up) breakout price patterns use Stop Market orders. The BOP (Breakout Pullback) can use Stop Market or Limit orders.

3TD Example(s):

March 3, 2010. CTs were bullish but not Unequivocally (first chart). The market began selling down from a fairly well-defined double-top. Two 3TD breakout trades are shown (3TD SHORT). The breakouts can also give BOP/EMA opportunities, and two of these are shown as secondary entries to the 3TD trades. Initial stop-loss on the 3TD breakout trades can make use of the 20-EMA line (just above).

March 26, 2010. The market never extended convincingly above the IBH on the YM (DJIA) e-mini. CTs were flat. This information means a trader might be looking to fade from a local maxima. Make sure the 20-EMA' (rate-of-change) is clearly negative when applying the 3TD SHORT. The 3TD breakout can look back to well-defined local minima as shown in the trade chart.

April 7, 2010. Extremely flat CTs occurred from the open and through the first hour of the session. If there is a well-defined 3TD price level to test, then it can be a high-probability trade.

March 3, 2010. Equivocal CTs. ES 1-min

March 3, 2010. 3TD Breakouts. ES 764-tick

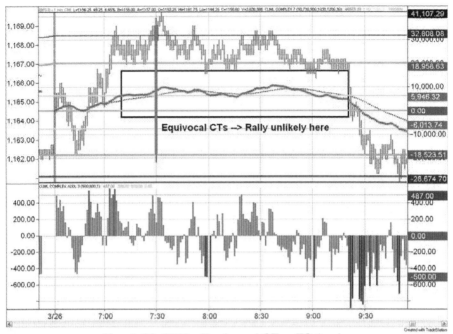

March 26, 2010. Equivocal CTs. ES 1-min

March 26, 2010. 3TD SHORT. YM 233-tick

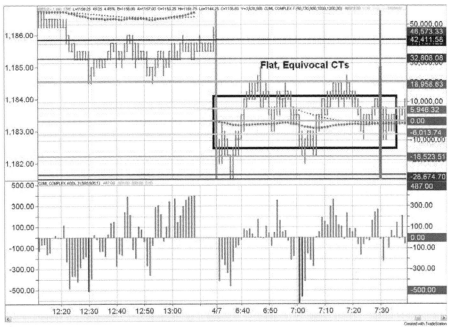

April 7, 2010. Flat, Equivocal CTs. ES 1-min

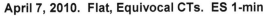

April 7, 2010. 3TD SHORT. ES 764-tick

3TU Example(s):

March 11, 2010. The ES contract extended above the IBH then, importantly, stayed in the upper third of the IB through the noon hour (NYSE). A 3TU LONG became a high probability trade following a second time up failure.

March 12, 2010. A daily review shows a strong NQ (Nasdaq-100) leader that recently exceeded a resistance level stretching back to the beginning of the year; see the NQ Daily chart. The IBL holds and there is a 3TU test. The NQ tick chart shows an ascending triangle. The 3TU price pattern off the IBL makes for a high probability trade.

April 6, 2010. CTs are bullish, the market became IBH Range Extended (IBH RE), tested the IBH on retracement, and remained above it moving into the afternoon rally period. These factors give the trader a bullish bias. A local 3TU price level offers an opportunity to use the 3TU LONG price pattern on the ES 764-tick chart.

March 11, 2010. 3TU LONG. ES 764-tick

March 12, 2010. NQ New Highs. NQ Daily

March 12, 2010. 3TU LONG. NQ 382-tick

April 6, 2010. CTs Bullish. ES 1-min

April 6, 2010. 3TU LONG. ES 764-tick

BOP Example(s):

March 25, 2010. CTs are bullish with the CTs histogram showing an almost complete lack of selling. Long entries are sought. When a 3TU breakout pullback remains above the 20-EMA, a BOP LONG trade sets up. Both the Limit and Stop Market order cases are shown.

The reader will justifiably question this example because here a 3TU LONG would likely have been stopped out. How is one to know when to use the 3TU or BOP LONG price pattern? The only answer is that trading is not a science and in this case a 3TU LONG, without a stop-loss level below the 20-EMA, was a trading loss that might have had to be endured.

April 15, 2010. The BOP trade is closely related to the EMA – both are retracement entries. The BOP can be a good entry when it is combined with a well-defined price level breakout. Two BOP SHORTs are shown in the chart.

Making sure the 20-EMA' (slope of the 20-EMA) is clearly positive or negative can help eliminate the failed breakout case, when the market head-fakes the trader with a breakout only to reverse. Using a Limit order with tight initial stop-loss or a Stop Market order with entry only when the market continues in the direction of the original breakout are two ways experienced traders lower their risk of loss from failed breakouts.

March 25, 2010. CTs Bullish. ES 1-min

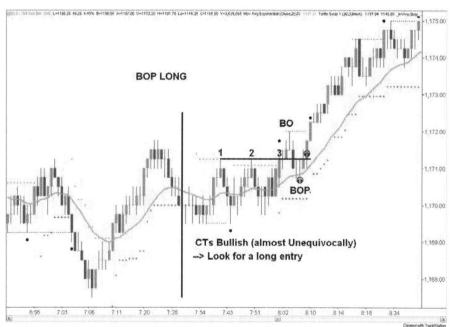

March 25, 2010. BOP LONG. ES 764-tick

April 15, 2010. BOP SHORT. ES 764-tick

Breakout Trades: IB Range Extension (Special Topic)

Initial Balance Range Extension (IB RE) is a breakout trade that enters the market following the first hour of trading. Two conditions must be met for the IB RE trade and there are three ways the trade can be entered.

The two signals which identify a possible IB RE Trend Trade, are:

- **IB Width**. A narrow IB indicates price congestion in the first hour of trading. Initial congestion can support a range breakout. The IB is reviewed against historical IB width data to determine a narrow IB.

- **Unequivocal CTs**. Unequivocal CTs indicate a market that is trending.

CTs can transition during the trading day from Equivocal to Unequivocal, and range extension may occur later in the trading day.

There are three ways to enter an IB RE trade:

1. With the initial extension breakout. A Stop Market order in the direction of the range extension can be used, one or two ticks beyond the IBH/L.
2. On retracement to IB extrema. This is a BOP price pattern trade.
3. On retracement to a 20-EMA using a 3-minute price chart. A near-term resting limit order is used, which takes its price from the 20-EMA.

Trend Days will often include an IB RE price move, and the Trend Trade examples, given previously, provide examples of trading IB RE.

While the IB RE trade may give better results when entered near the IB (shortly after the first hour), IB RE can occur later in the morning or afternoon. IB RE may occur as the result of an afternoon rally.

Reversal Trades

Reversal trades, often referred to as fading the market, consist of three essential components:

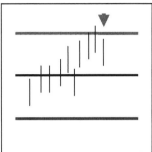

1. **Equivocal CTs**. If CTs are Unequivocal, indicating a Trend Day, then reversals that are more than short-term scalps have a lower probability of success. Trend Days should be traded in the direction of the trend using local retracement entries.

2. **Price Level**. It is important to have a price level against which to set a reversal trade.

3. **Price Pattern**. Trading a price pattern improves the reversal setup and helps to ease the sense that one is catching a falling knife with a reversal setup. The price patterns used to trade reversals are: 3TF and PDT SHORT and RHS LONG.

In addition, a technical indicator of price extension is useful to confirm a reversal decision. The MACD helps the trader estimate overbought/oversold (OB/OS) conditions when a reversal is attempted. The CTs help determine that a Trend Day is not in progress, so that an OB/OS technical indication is useful information when considering a reversal setup. A technical indicator by itself is never reliable enough to completely define trade setups, but it does offer additional information that can be used to help confirm trades.

Because reversal trades in general are risky, as one is betting on the market turning, the use of automated stop-loss and fast exit profit-targets is crucial. The goal is to get the trade to a no-lose configuration as quickly as possible and then, if we are lucky, see the market actually reverse for a larger winning runner possibility. Again, stop-loss and profit-target guidelines are given in the Trade Management chapter.

The Very Latest E-Mini Trading

Example(s):

April 24, 2008. Long NQ contract from the IBL, S1 and PDL. The CTs were Equivocal and based on them, the 10 point ES sell-off in the morning was not supported by market internals (it may have been largely due to the day's opening gap). The IB was wide, relative to the previous 100 day average, and the IBL, S1 and PDL all coincided. This made for quite an extraordinary setup and begged to be taken.

The knowledgeable and aggressive trader would have entered with more than his or her usual number of contracts. I executed the trade, but without the full conviction it called for. An actual account log is shown here. Note the use of a fast exit profit-target on the first two of the three original contracts. The third contract was held as a winning runner. Trailing stop-loss eventually closed the position (the final stop market order shown)[5].

Filled/Canceled	Symbol	Type	Qty Filled	Stop	Limit	Filled Price	Order#
4/24/2008 7:37	NQM08	Buy	3		1893.50	1893.50	1-2017-6939
4/24/2008 7:38	NQM08	Sell	1		1894.50	1894.50	1-2017-7504
4/24/2008 7:39	NQM08	Sell	1		1895.00	1895.00	1-2017-7842
4/24/2008 8:55	NQM08	Sell	1	1926.75	Market	1926.50	1-2017-7150

April 24, 2008. Long NQ Trade Detail

December 4, 2008. Short from the Previous Day's High (PDH). CTs are Equivocal so that a short fade from a price maxima is the objective. Because the IBH closely coincided with the PDH, that price level made for a compelling entry price.

Two trade entries are noted on the chart; in fact, both would have been winning trades. The first entry is aggressive trading. The second entry follows the PDT price pattern.

---

[5] The NQM08 (NQ e-mini, June 2008 expiration) contract prices and NQ continuous contract chart prices shown here do not match. Continuous contract charts are a concatenation of quarterly futures contracts with price corrections made relative to the latest contract price. They relieve the trader from having to specify contract month when reviewing charts over lengthy periods of time. TradeStation continuous contracts are specified with the '@' sign. For example, @NQ is the continuous NQ e-mini contract.

184

April 24, 2008. CTs Equivocal

April 24, 2008. NQ Long. NQ 3-min

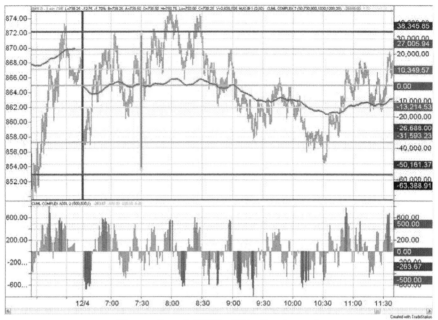

December 4, 2008. CTs Equivocal

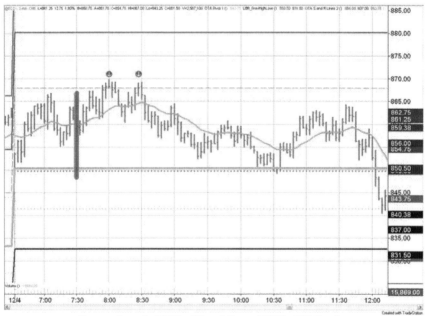

December 4, 2008. Short from PDH. ES 3-min

December 8, 2009. PDT SHORT. Short from an Opening Gap Closure. See the Trade Basics chapter for a discussion of opening gap closure. As long as the CTs are not indicating a Trend Day, the gap closure trade can be high probability.

February 26, 2010. RHS LONG. Long from 1100, which is an extremely Big Number (BN). The trade represents all views of the market coming together to promote a long entry:

- CTs were bullish (Day-Type)
- The market held above the huge 1100 BN (Price Level)
- The MACD had recently been near a 2-sigma oversold level (Technical Indication of Price Extension)
- The time-of-day was just prior to the afternoon rally period (Time-of-Day)
- An RHS pattern formed that could be used for trade entry.

March 29, 2010. 3TF SHORT. The CTs were very flat. Three attempts to range extend the IBH failed. With CTs so flat, a low-risk entry (stop-loss just above the IBH level) was possible.

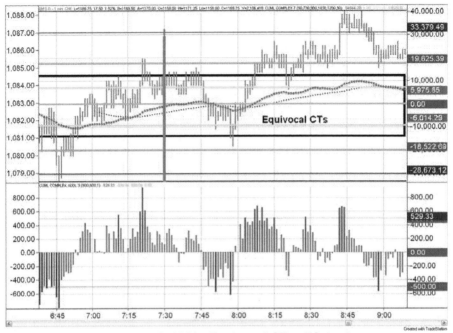

December 8, 2010. Equivocal CTs. ES 1-min

December 8, 2010. Opening Gap Closure. NQ 3-min

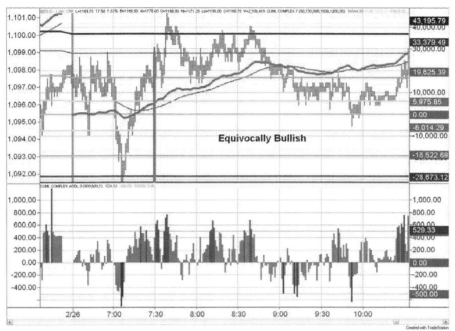

February 26, 2010. CTs Bullish. ES 1-min

February 26, 2010. 1100 BN, MACD OS and RHS LONG. ES 764-tick

March 29, 2010. CTs Flat and Equivocal. ES 1-min

March 29, 2010. 3TF SHORT from IBH. NQ 382-tick

Reversal Trades: Initial Balance Reversal (Special Topic)

An Initial Balance Reversal (IB Reversal) trade fades the market assuming a price reversal back into the first hour's trading range. There are three components to the setup.

1. **IB Width.** The wider the IB the better is the chance that the first hour saw some price discovery and the market will remain within the IB. The IB is compared against historical IB width data to determine its relative width.

2. **Equivocal CTs.** Equivocal CTs support the market remaining within the IB. While it is difficult to read CTs from just the first hour's trading, CTs which remain below the first hour historical level indicate Equivocal CTs. Equivocal CTs indicate the day may unfold as not a Trend day. Unequivocal CTs will have a steady and regular slope and should not be faded (unless the trader is scalping).

3. **IBH or IBL are at a Key Price Level.** If the IBH or IBL are at the Previous Day's High or Low (PDH or PDL), Support S1/2 or Resistance R1/2 the setup is stronger.

The IB Reversal trade is entered using a limit order at the IB extrema plus (long) or minus (short) a small (2-3) tick offset. The PDT price pattern is often used to enter.

Example(s):

January 13, 2009. Short from the IBH. The IB width was somewhat less than the average. The CTs were muted implying rotation and supported fading. The IBH was the Day's Previous High (DPH) at the time of the trade. Note that an IB Reversal trade does not have to be made immediately after the IB is established (after the first hour of trading); however, the IB loses some of its relevance by the afternoon session.

January 27, 2009. Long from the IBL. The IB width was just short of its 100 day average. The CTs were muted through the first hour and Equivocally bullish overall. A long entry was made from a double-bottom retracement to the IBL

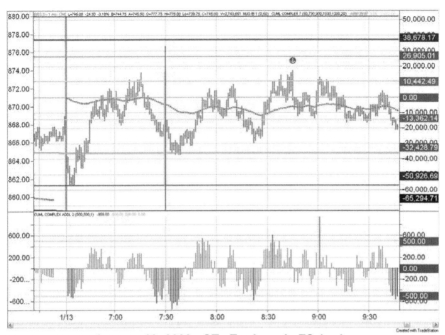

January 13, 2009. CTs Equivocal. ES 1-min

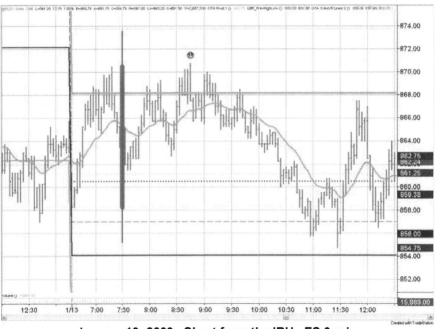

January 13, 2009. Short from the IBH. ES 3-min

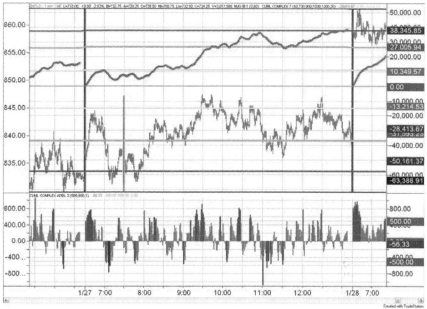

January 27, 2009. CTs Equivocally Bullish. ES 1-min

January 27, 2009. Long from the IBL. ES 3-min

Divergence Trades

Divergence Trades cover a class of trading that seeks to find technical divergences, or discrepencies, which can be exploited by the trader. The trader simulataneously reviews multiple inputs looking for divergence conditions that normally should not occur, with the expectation that the market will revert to a state where the divergence no longer exists. Trades are taken based on this normalizing expectation.

Three divergences were mentioned in the Trading Basics chapter: CTs-Price; MACD-Price and Inter-Market. There are trade setups for each of these divergences.

CTs-Price Divergence

The CTs-Price Divergence trade seeks to exploit subtle divergences between recent futures pricing and readings from the NYSE Ticks. Is current futures price action supported by the broader underlying stock market?

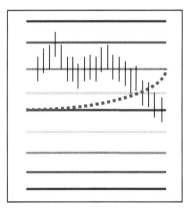

One of the most difficult questions the active day-trader must answer is whether price action in the opposite direction of a trend is the beginning of a reversal or a short-term retracement that offers a new opportunity to enter with the trend.

CTs-Price divergence is a tool that can help answer the difficult question. In this sense, the CTs-Price Divergence setup can be considered as type of trend-following trade, as well.

Example(s):

April 16, 2010. The market has broken through a very key BN price level of 1200, which was the IBL, and sold down to near the 1192 level before retracing back to previous support near 1198 (the two-point BN phenomenon?). But the 5.25 point retracement, a price move that is not insignificant by intra-day standards, is accompanied by a very weak CTs reading. See the rectangle enclosing the CTs histogram in the example charts. As a result, the retracement is most likely not part of an unfolding 'V' reversal but a local retracement unsupported by broader stock market buying. It represents a possible retracement short entry to get on the larger selloff.

A BOP SHORT price pattern entry can be used from the 1198 level. The trader may want to use the 1200 level in his stop-loss calculation, setting intial stop-loss just above it.

Later, in the same session, we see another case of CTs-Price Divergence. Once again, NYSE Ticks accumulation does not show any buying during a retracement that we might otherwise consider as the beginning of a reversal. A double-top makes for a good entry in the direction of the day's selling.

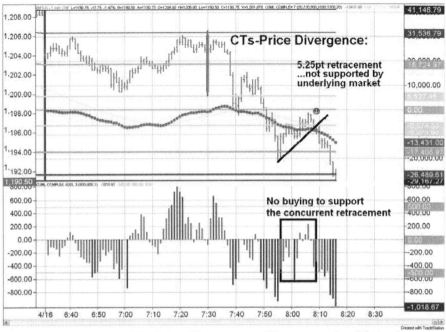

April 16, 2010. CTs-Price Divergence. First example. ES 1-min

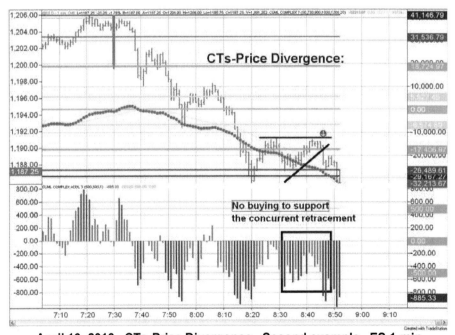

April 16, 2010. CTs-Price Divergence. Second example. ES 1-min

MACD-Price Divergence

MACD-Price Divergence was described in the Trading Basics chapter. It is a surprisingly simple and effective technical trade setup[6].

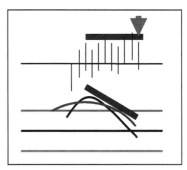

MACD Overbought (OB) and Oversold (OS) levels are pertinent when the market is not trending. When a trend is underway, the OB and OS conditions offer little information that can be traded. Thus, the MACD is used in conjunction with the CTs day-type determination.

The MACD-Price Divergence setup is used with Statistical MACD(12, 26, 9) parameters (see Trading Basics) and primarily with tick charts.

With the Statistical MACD, the OB/OS levels are a number of standard deviations and 2-sigma values are currently used (two standard deviations).

MACD-Price Divergences can occur without the MACD having achieved the OB/OS state completely, and these can still be reliable trading signals.

The MACD-Price Divergence trade can be entered using one of the pre-defined price patterns.

---

[6] The 2nd Edition of the book gives a little less attention to MACD-Price Divergence than the 1st Edition, even as there has been recent work to move to a statistical MACD implementation (see the Trading Basics chapter). The MACD-Price Divergence setup remains valid, but it has fallen lower down the list of trade setups that are used. The MACD continues to be a favorite indicator for gauging price extension and as a guide to keep the trader aligned with intra-day price moves.

Example(s):

December 3, 2009. A number of conditions occur to motivate a good trade in the NQ contract:

- CTs are Equivocal – we are not in the midst of a Trend Day and the market may be faded, long or short.
- The IB is relatively wide and the market holds at the IBL with an RHS price pattern.
- A MACD-Price Divergence sets up.

December 17, 2009. A well-defined double-top coincides with a 2-sigma MACD OB and MACD-Price divergence.

March 3, 2010. Here is an application of the MACD-Price Divergence setup, used in conjunction with the 3TF SHORT price pattern. The triple top failure was re-inforced by a 2-sigma MACD OB condition and price divergence.

December 3, 2009. Equivocal CTs. ES 1-min

December 3, 2009. MACD-Price Divergence with RHS LONG. NQ 382-tick

December 17, 2009. MACD-Price Divergence with PDT SHORT. NQ 382-tick

March 3, 2010. MACD-Price Divergence with 3TF SHORT. TF 233-tick

Inter-Market Divergence

Inter-Market Divergence makes use of the four widely traded and related e-mini stock index futures markets simultaneously (ES, TF, NQ, YM). When one of the markets diverges significantly from the others, then there may be a trading opportunity.

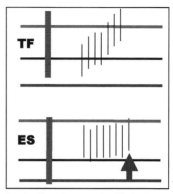

A leader and follower interpretation categorizes the Russell 2000 (e-mini TF) as a leader to the follower S&P 500 (e-mini ES), and the Nasdaq 100 (e-mini NQ) as a leader to the follower DJIA (e-mini YM). In this model, as an example, if the Day-Type is indicating a bullish bias and the TF contract is rallying, while the ES contract remains in a consolidation pattern, then a long position in the ES contract can be considered.

The Inter-Market Divergence (IMD) trade is typically entered with a Limit order at a price that is close to the market. When the divergence is detected it is often the case that the trader will want to establish a position immediately. In order that the market is not chased one of the price patterns can be used.

Example(s):

December 22, 2008. Short YM. CTs are Equivocally bearish. We hope to find a short entry. The NQ contract is at S1 and the YM contract is well above it and retracing to its Open price. Meanwhile, the TF contract, which should be a leader is flat around S1 and making no signs of moving higher. We use the YM 233-tick chart to enter when price moved back to a local maximum and the MACD is OB. A 3TF topping pattern made for a reliable short entry with low-risk intial stop-loss just above the top.

January 28, 2009. Long YM. The CTs are Unequivocally bullish and we are looking for a long entry. The YM contract is lagging all other markets, consolidating over the lunch hour at R1 with ES, TF and NQ far above R1, and, in fact, TF continues a steady rally throughout. We want to be long prior to possible afternoon continuation rally and make use of a well-defined buying ledge and subsequent EMA retracement to enter. The buying ledge gives a low-risk entry because intial stop-loss can be set just under it.

March 25, 2009. Long NQ. It is amazing how much divergence can occur between the four related e-mini stock index futures.

In this example, the CTs were Unequivocally bullish after a much better than expected Durable Goods economic report released 30 minutes before the open. The ES, TF and YM were all heading higher after an opening gap up (5 points in the ES contract). Curiously, the NQs, which were recently a strong leader, showing bullishness during the current bear market rally, are lagging. In the chart below, the NQ contract is almost flat while the other contracts are showing definite upward movement. If both leaders, TF and NQ were divergent from the followers, ES and YM, then one might assume ES and YM were overbought. Here, only NQ trails. The consolidation buying ledge formed by the NQs makes for an excellent entry. The Unequivocally bullish CTs strongly supported the long entry.

A long trade was executed with 3x contracts using a limit order of 1248.00 immediately following a short-term retracement to the 20-EMA. The two tier fast exit contracts were automatically closed for 6 and 10 tick profits; trailing stops exited the final tier at 1257.00.

December 22, 2008. CTs Equivocally Bearish

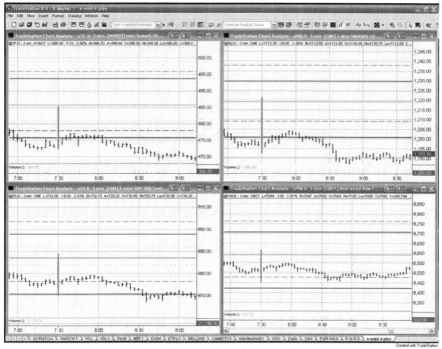

December 22, 2008. NQ at S2 and YM above S1

December 22, 2008. YM Short. YM 233-tick

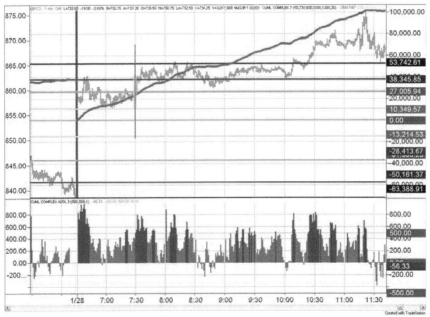

January 28, 2009. CTs Unequivocally Bullish

January 28, 2009. YM at R1 and NQ above R2

January 28, 2009. YM Long. YM 233-tick

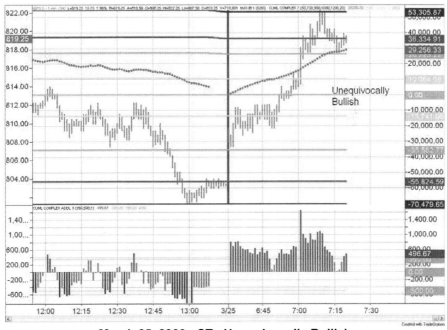

Unequivocally
Bullish

March 25, 2009. CTs Unequivocally Bullish

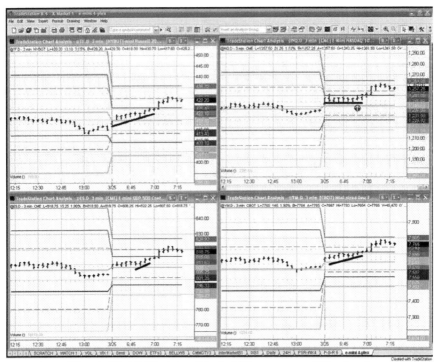

March 25, 2009. Inter-Market Divergence: NQ. 3-min

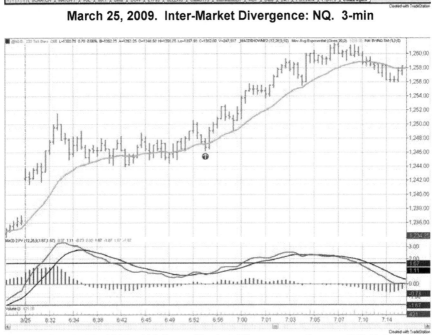

March 25, 2009. NQ Inter-Market Divergence Long. NQ tick

Market Profile Trades

The trade setups so far have used the Market Profile Initial Balance (IB) extensively. We can expand the use of the Market Profile with trade setups that are based on its Value Area (VA) definition.

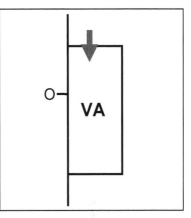

The Market Profile VA represents a 70% price action range centered about the mode price of a session (most frequent price and called the "Point of Control," POC, in the Market Profile theory). In a normal distribution, one standard deviation contains approximately 70% of the data, so the VA has a statistical basis to it – a data point that is further than one standard deviation from a data sample's average begins to approach "outlier" status.

In descriptions of Market Profile VA trade techniques, the term VA refers specifically to the previous session's Value Area, and it is a fixed and objective range based on the mode plus 70% definition[7]. The term *Developing VA* refers to the current session VA, as it is being built by the day's active trading. The Developing VA, or DVA, can change throughout a session, and estimating the extent of the DVA is similar to estimating whether the DPH and DPL (Day's Previous High and Low) will hold until the end of a session.

Finally, as mentioned earlier, and similar to the IBH and IBL, there are VAH, VAL, DVAH and DVAL price levels marking the Value Area and Developing Value Area Highs and Lows.

In designing VA trade setups, there are four basic types of VA-relative (and DVA-relative) price action that can be considered:

---

[7] There are cases where a session's price distribution contains two modes and those modes are a significant distance apart. This often gives rise to a double-distribution profile with two equally populated VAs. The session's closing price will often determine which mode and VA are most relevant going into the next session. There are also cases where a session's price distribution is so long and thin that the VA gives little information. These distributions are based on very wide range "outside" days.

- Price opens within the VA and stays within it;
- Price opens within the VA and moves beyond it;
- Price opens outside the VA and moves back into it; and
- Price opens outside the VA and stays beyond it.

Case I. Price Opens Within the VA and Stays Within. When price begins within a VA we might expect it to remain there, because the VA represents a one standard deviation price range. If the day is not a Trend Day, then we might rely on the VAH/L as early price extrema (resistance and support) for the new session and fade the market when it moves to either of these levels. Later in the session, the DVAH/L will replace the VAH/L as extrema references.

There is something referred to as the "80% Rule" in Market Profile trading. The 80% Rule proposes that if price moves back into a VA and remains there for two consecutive 30 minute periods – two TPOs, then there is an 80% chance that it will move across the breadth of the VA as a case of market rotation[8]. If price opens within the VA, then executes price discovery just outside it, only to retrace back into the VA, the 80% Rule may apply.

Case II. Price Opens Within the VA and Moves Beyond. Price opens similarly to the previous case but then extends outside the VA. This is similar to the IB Range Extension concept. It is a breakout condition which can be traded with Stop Market orders just above/below the VAH/L or with BOP (Breakout Pullback) Limit orders at the VAH/L, should the market temporarily retrace to these levels following the initial breakout.

Case III. Price Opens Outside the VA and Moves Back In. The previous session closed outside its VA or overnight trading took the market outside it. In this case, the VA, defining 70% of the previous sessions trading range, acts as a sort of magnet pulling price back to a previously defined area of value. The 80% Rule applies to this case.

Case IV. Price Opens Outside the VA and Stays Beyond. The new session opens similarly to the previous case, outside of the previous session's VA. With the opening price above or below the VA, as in Case III, the trader closely watches to see if it retraces back to the VAH/L. If the market rejects further movement back into the VA, then this can be

---

[8] I do not know of any back-test data that corroborates the claim.

an opportunity to enter on a retracement. Alternatively, the market drives off its open, never retracing to the VA. The Market Profile theory refers to this as "Open Drive."

The VA-relative price action cases are depicted in the following schematics[9]. There certainly are other valid setups based on the Market Profile definitions. Those here represent the most well-known VA-based setups. Quantitative back-test results are not available currently (at least as far as this author can determine). The 'O' label in the schematics stands for the session open price level.

Following these schematic overviews, specific Market Profile VA trade examples are given.

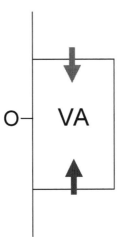

VA Price Action – Case I: VAH/L Fade

---

[9] The VAs depicted are based on the previous session. The price action depicted – the Open price and schematic price bars – represents current session price action.

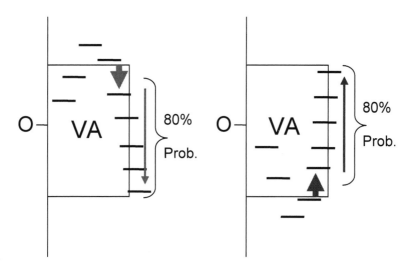

VA Price Action – Case I/80% Rule: VAH/L Fade

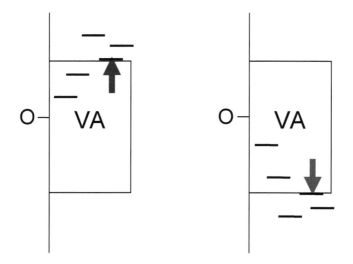

VA Price Action – Case II: VAH/L Breakout and BOP

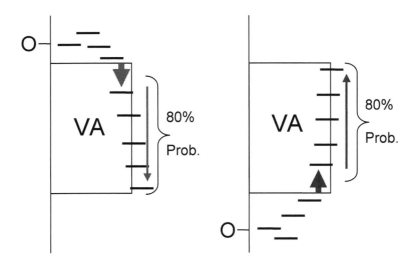

VA Price Action – Case III/80% Rule: VAH/L Trend-Following

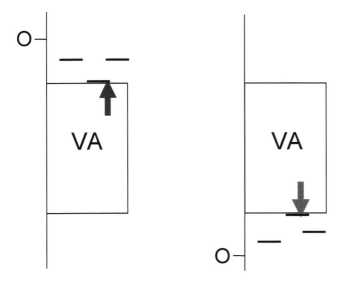

VA Price Action – Case IV: VAH/L BOP

Example(s):

July 16, 2009. The trade from July 16th[10] illustrates how a number of market views combined to make for a high probability trade. ES opened within the VA, and the VAH was the previous day's high. When the first hour of the session showed Equivocal CTs (non-trending day), a short from the VAH made for a good trade. This example is a Case I trade.

April 16, 2010. If the relevant Market Profile setup had been followed it would have made for a stellar result. The market opened below VA, retraced back up to within exactly two ticks of the VAL, and then sold off sharply from there. Typically, a two tick offset from the relevant price level is used in setting Limit orders. This example is a Case IV trade.

May 11, 2010. ES opens just below VAL with an opening gap down and then immediately begins to close the gap, moving up into the VA (previous session's VA – May 10). As the 80% Rule predicts, the market then traversed the entire width of the VA, and continued higher. At this point, the CTs are showing a very bullish day, the opening gap was closed, IBH RE occurred and the VAH exceeded. A retracement long from the VAH made for a well-defined Market Profile trade. Two trade entries are shown: A Buy Stop just above the VAH and a Limit on retracement to the VAH. Both are good entries. These trades fall into Case III, with entries after the full width of the VA was traversed (80% Rule). An astute Market Profile day-trader might have entered when the VA was first entered, earlier in the session, relying on the 80% Rule.

---

[10] This example was first published in a <u>Futures Magazine</u> article, Dec. 2009.

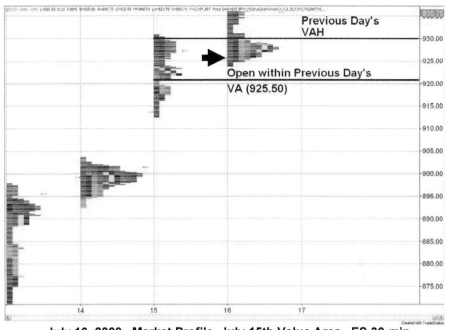

July 16, 2009. Market Profile, July 15th Value Area. ES 30-min

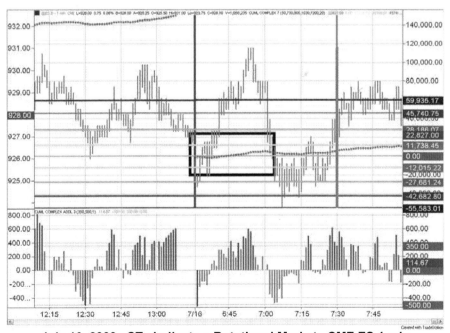

July 16, 2009. CTs Indicate a Rotational Market. CME ES 1-min

July 16, 2009. ES Price Levels. CME ES 3-Min

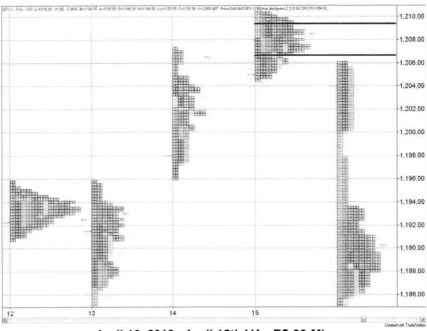

April 16, 2010. April 15th VA. ES 30-Min

April 16, 2010. VAL Retracement Short. ES 3-min

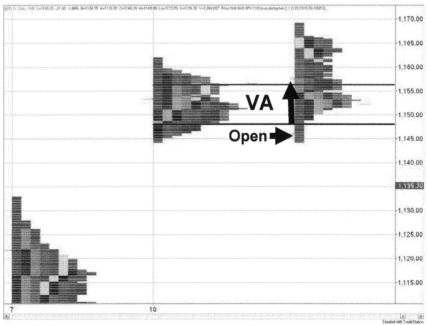

May 11, 2010. May 10th VA. ES 30-Min

May 11, 2010. CTs Bullish to Unequivocally Bullish. ES 1-min

May 11, 2010. VAH Breakout and Retracement Longs. ES 3-min

Time-of-Day Trading

We can combine the trade setups with Time-of-Day to better address how to trade during a session. This gives form to the trading day and helps to limit the amount of time the trader spends in front of screens.

Based on the eight periods in the table, below, the trader is free to pick a subset on which to focus his or her trading. For example, I typically concentrate on First half-hour, First hour (IB), a possible Afternoon Rally (after 12:30pm), one or two trades from the Afternoon Pivots, and the Last Hour.

Time	Description	Trading Relevance
9:30am	Stock market opens	Market opening gap offers first trade opportunity. (Note: Opening gap trades are not currently defined by the trading system. Opening gap *closure* may be a high probability trade.)
10:00am	First half-hour pivot	Market can reverse. 10:00am economic reports can create, or contribute to, a pivot.
10:30am	First hour pivot. Initial Balance complete	Trades based on the first hour Initial Balance possible. Market can reverse from IB extrema or follow-through with IB RE (Range Extension).
11:30am	Morning session ending	Lunch-time congestion makes new trades problematic until the afternoon session. Traders need to be aware of lunch-time chop that is often unproductive.
12:30pm	Pre-cursor to afternoon session	Lunch-time is half over. Begin to look for signs of afternoon session activity. Rallies often begin between 12:30 and 1:30pm. This can be a tough time to short.
1:30pm (2:00pm 2:30pm)	Afternoon pivot "Minor" pivots	Mid-way point between the start of the afternoon (12:00pm) and the start of the last hour (3:00pm). If an afternoon rally is to occur, it likely will have begun by the 1:30pm pivot. Market can sometimes make reversals on PM 30 minute "minor" pivots.
3:00pm 3:30pm	Last-hour pivot Last half-hour pivot	Sudden reversals may occur at the beginning of the last hour or the beginning of the last half-hour.
3:50pm	Session ending	No new trades opened. Erratic behavior possible prior to 4:00pm stock market close.

Time-of-Day Trades

Summary

High probability trades become possible when a variety of independent market perspectives are used to define setups. The e-mini stock index futures system described in this text attempts to coordinate five market views to identify high probability trades:

- Day-Type
- Price Level
- Technical Indication
- Time-of-Day
- Price Patterns

.
When multiple market views are incorporated in a trade setup the chance of success improves.

The five market views and the various setups may at first appear over-whelming: How is the discretionary trader expected to integrate this amount of information, and in real-time? By watching the market daily and using automated indicators to help identify trade setups, the trader becomes adept at identifying trading opportunities.

It is my experience that the trader who makes rash entry decisions, chasing the market excitedly trying to get in on quick profits, will not generally be profitable. The trader who uses various market views and well-defined trade setups – planning trade entries ahead of price action and anticipating the market – has a better chance of success. See the Trade Examples chapter for additional material pertaining to discretionary trade psychology.

In the next chapter, trade management will be the focus. After describing the stop-loss and profit-target options available, the details of trade entry and exit will be automated. This allows the trader to save valuable energy and focus on identifying trade setups.

Trade Management

Once the trader pulls the trigger on a trade setup and enters the market the work of managing the trade begins. The trader must determine how to exit a trade profitably or, if the trade moves against him, then with as little loss as possible.

Because of the intra-day volatility of the stock market, most, if not all, seasoned traders advocate a strict use of stop-loss when trading stock index futures. This fact means there should be no single large loss to endure and is one of the attractions of the e-mini day-trading experience.

This chapter covers many facets of managing an e-mini position. Topics include:

- How and when to scale out profits.
- Getting to a no-lose, on-the-house position where the trader has the opportunity of possibly realizing a winning runner without the risk of loss.
- Staying in a position to realize a winning runner.

Experienced traders know that almost as important as the initial trade setup and entry is the management of an open position, and this chapter covers this key area. In particular, two new approaches are introduced:

- A directed graph model is used to calculate a position's expected value. These models quantify, for the first time, the profit and loss properties of a trade management strategy.
- A hybrid trading desktop that automates trade management tasks. Trade management automation eliminates potentially costly trading errors, provides the means to implement automated stop-loss and fast exit profit-targets, and creates a framework to realize winning runners.

The chapter begins with an analysis of various stop-loss and profit-target strategies for managing a position entered using the trade setups of the last chapter. By analyzing alternative strategies we are able to provide guidelines for managing trades; that is, specifically when to execute stop-loss and profit-target orders.

This analysis came about as I was confronted with a variety of trade management strategies in the media and wanted to quantify their outcomes. The analysis provides a recommendation of how to best handle e-mini trades without simply saying, "Do it this way because it works."

Because reversal trades make up a large number of setups in the e-mini stock index futures system, it is important to automate stop-loss and profit-target execution. That is, while the setups lead to high probability trades, it is also the case that a significant number of reversal trades will fail, and they can fail quickly.

Given that price level is a key component of a reversal trade, when a trade is entered with a limit order it is likely that a small reversal from the entry price will occur. With software automation, a fast exit profit-target from the initial reversal can be realized, and that profit will serve to offset any losses should the reversal ultimately fail. But, should the reversal occur, then there is the opportunity to realize a winning runner from the remaining open contracts.

In summary, automation seeks to book quick profits that can be used to establish a no-risk position for the remaining winning runner contracts. This is the ultimate goal of a scale-out trade management strategy.

Following the strategy analysis, the specific tools used to implement the stop-loss and profit-target automation are described. This will include a description of order entry execution as well as tools for remaining in trades to capture a winning runner.

When the trade setups of the previous chapter are combined with trade management strategies and practices, a complete e-mini stock index futures trading system is realized.

Directed Graphs and Expected Value

In broadest terms, there are essentially two trade management strategies: All in/all out and scaled. Either technique can be used for scalping, where a few contract ticks are garnered per trade, or for a trade that may last for a larger portion of the trading session.

The all in/all out strategy is a one-punch trade with the goal of getting a single trade decision correct, while the scaled strategy uses subsets, or tiers, of an original position to take off profits quickly, moderately quickly, or over a fairly lengthy period during the day. At the heart of the scaled strategy is the desire to reduce risk and retain a number of winning runner contracts that can be held at no cost to the trader and which may take advantage of a significant intra-day rally or sell-off. There are both scale-in and scale-out variations to scaled trade management.

The e-mini system advocates scaled trade management. However, because of the variation possible with the scaled approach, scaled strategies can be difficult to analyze. What is done is to compare well-known scaled strategies using directed graphs and expected value calculations based on those graphs. This quantifies the expected value of each strategy, and we are better able to apply scaled strategies to our trading.

A description of the Directed Graph and Expected Value method begins with a simple coin toss example. Imagine a $1 coin is flipped. Heads you win; tails you lose. What is your return from the coin flip?

We know there is a 50-50 chance of winning when fairly tossing an unbiased coin: A 50% chance of heads and a 50% chance of tails. A slightly more mathematical way of describing this is to say that there is a 0.5 probability of heads occurring and a $1 - 0.5 = 0.5$ probability of tails occurring. A player's return is then calculated as the probability of his or her outcome multiplied by the value of the outcome. In the case of the coin flip, $0.50 \times \$1 = \$0.50$. A player's return on any toss is, in theory, $0.50, one half of the $1 coin.

The Expected Value of a game or probability experiment is defined as the sum of each possible outcome multiplied by the probability of the outcome. In the coin flip example, the expected value calculation is $0.50 \times \$1$ (Heads) $+ 0.50 \times \$1$ (Tails) $= \$0.50 + \$0.50 = \$1$. Someone walks away with the dollar coin, either the person calling heads or the person calling tails.

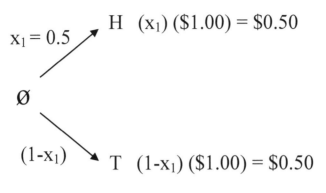

Coin Flip Directed Graph

A Directed Graph model of this is shown in the above figure, Coin Flip Directed Graph. The ø character indicates an initial state before the toss of the coin. Because there are only two outcomes from the initial state, Heads or Tails, there are only two paths, or arrows, from the initial state, one for the Heads outcome and one for the Tails outcome. (Directed graphs where from each state just two events are possible are called Binary Directed Graphs. Trade analysis uses binary directed graphs.)

In the coin flip directed graph, the probability of the Heads event is labeled x_1, and has a value of 0.50. The probability of the Tails event, or not Heads, is $1 - x_1$, and also has a value of 0.50. The value of each outcome is its probability of occurrence multiplied by the value outcome of the occurrence. Each terminal state of the directed graph has a value calculation. The expected value for the entire game is the sum of all the terminal values.

While the graph is not needed for the simple coin flip example, when more complicated games are studied, the directed graph works well to organize outcomes. In particular, directed graphs work well for organizing the outcomes and expected value from scaled trade management strategies.

Basic Trade Management

A basic unscaled trade management strategy has exactly the same directed graph as the coin flip. The only differences is the value used for x_1 and the different values the market takes at the end of the trade – these will be the stop-loss and profit-target values used in the trade. For the coin flip x_1 has a 50% probability, or 0.50. For the unscaled trade strategy x_1 will be the probability of a winning trade and is a model input. Similarly, stop-loss and profit-target values are inputs to the model.

The figure Basic Trade Management Directed Graph gives the directed graph for the basic unscaled trade management strategy. $\varnothing$ is the initial state before the market is entered. x_1 is the probability of a winning trade. SL_1 is the stop-loss price, as a number of ticks from the entry price. PT_1 is the profit-target price, also a number of ticks from the entry price.

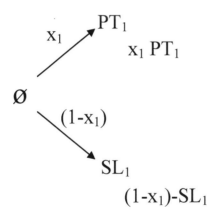

Basic Trade Management Directed Graph

A winning trade occurs when a profit-target is reached before a stop-loss. The probability of a winning trade is closely related to the prices used for profit-target and stop-loss. For example, if one's stop-loss is too close to a position's entry price, then typically the probability of a winning trade is low. Traders know this phenomenon from the experience of setting their stops too tightly and getting prematurely stopped out. Conversely, if one's stop-loss is large compared to the profit-target, then the probability of a winning trade increases. In theory, one can approach a 100% winning trade percentage by making the stop-loss large compared to the profit-target. Automated strategy testers see this phenomenon when a high winning percentage is achieved in strategy back-test if wide stops and small profit-targets are used. Of course, in practice, trade psychology and account margin must be considered, so that allowing overly large stop-loss is infeasible.

In the case of the ES contract, experienced traders, unless executing extremely fast scalping, typically use an initial stop-loss value of at least two points (8 ticks). There is typically enough jitter in the market that initial stops cannot be set tighter. Actual price action data can be used to help determine SL_1.

The Table ES Example ATR Data, gives recent "Average True Range"[1] data for the ES contract. From the sample it is seen that the contract moves through a range of approximately four points in 10 minutes. Assuming a trade to one side of the market (long or short), we can expect, on average, a two point price move against a new position in ten minutes. This helps explain the trader's desire to allow at least two points of wiggle room. There will be trade setups when less than a two point intial stop-loss can be used. For example, in some cases, if the market breaches a well defined ledge, then a failed trade might be assumed. In this case, it may be possible to lower the two point stop-loss rule. But a two point stop-loss is a reasonable initial boundary condition in the ES directed graph models[2].

(For the other e-mini contracts, make use of their roughly equivalent tick-to-index values to compute an intial stop-loss value. For example, a two point ES value gives a 20 point YM value; a 3.5 – 4.0 point NQ value; and a 1.5 TF value.)

Once the two point SL_1 value is determined, the PT_1 and x_1 values can be tested. A baseline model sets $PT_1 = SL_1$ (= 2 points = 8 ticks) and

---

[1] Average True Range (ATR) is a measure of price dispersion which takes into account bar chart interval gaps, thus giving a truer measure of price movement averaged across bars. See the excellent text, <u>Trading Systems and Methods</u>, Perry J. Kaufman, John Wiley & Sons. Data shown represents ATR over the past year using the intervals shown.

[2] During periods of increased market volatility, the number of contracts traded may need to be reduced and stops widened.

tests various values of x_1. Rule-of-thumb x_1 values, assuming trade setups are valid, take a range of 67% - 80%; i.e., a range of 2-of-3 to 4-of-5 trades are winners. The trader can paper-trade proposed trade setups with a simulator and collect x_1 data based on SL_1 and PT_1.

When a trade strategy directed graph is drawn with stop-loss, profit-target and win-loss probabilities, it is a straight-forward exercise to assign outcomes to the termination nodes. Summing the outcomes produces a trade profit and loss expected value. A spreadsheet easily accommodates the exercise and provides the flexibility to alter trade inputs in order to study possible outcomes.

Mins	ATR Mean	ATR StdDev
1	1.43	0.69
3	2.46	1.24
5	3.16	1.61
10	4.37	2.28
30	7.01	3.77
60	9.14	5.12
120	10.42	6.22
240	10.85	7.79

ES ATR Example Data

Table Trade Management Strategy Profit and Loss 1, gives the results for the basic strategy. In the table, SL_1 = 8 (ticks), PT_1 = SL_1, and x_1 = 70%. The strategy expected value sum, labeled as P&L (Profit and Loss) is given in ticks. A final entry, P&L/CARS[3], gives a relative measure of the profitability of the strategy when contract margin is considered. The P&L/CARS divides the P&L value by the maximum number of contracts held as part of the strategy and is used to compare different strategy results.

Note that the minimal number of contracts is used to calculate expected value. In the basic strategy, this is referred to as "1x contracts" where x

---

[3] CARS – a nickname for contracts used by futures traders.

is any whole number. Multiply the value *x* by the spreadsheet result to obtain an absolute expected value P&L. For example, if the trader was opening a position with five contracts (*x*=5), then the expected value P&L for the strategy would be 3.2 x 5 = 16 ticks.

The basic unscaled strategy serves as a baseline against which more elaborate management strategies are compared.

Inputs

1st P-T Win% (X1)	70%
1st P-T Ticks (PT1)	8
1st S-L Ticks (SL1)	8

Strategies

1	SL1	PT1	P&L	P&L /CARS
	-2.40	5.60	3.20	3.20

Trade Management Strategy Profit and Loss 1

2-Tiered Scale Strategy

A 2-Tiered scale-out strategy is commonly promoted in the media. A position is entered with 2*x* contracts. An initial stop-loss order is placed above (short position) or below (long position) the trade entry price using a stop-market order for the entire 2*x* contracts. A first, or fast exit, profit-target price for half the position (1*x* contracts) is pre-determined and executed with a limit order or manually by the trader with a market order when the profit-target price is touched.

If the initial stop-loss is first executed, then the trade completes for a loss. If the first profit-target is reached, 1*x* contracts are closed for an initial fast exit profit. A second stop-loss is then placed as a new stop-market order for the remaining 1*x* contracts. The second stop-loss price is often set at or near the position's original entry price so that a no-risk or slightly profitable position is realized. A second profit-target price, again at a pre-determined price may then be entered or, alternatively, a trailing stop

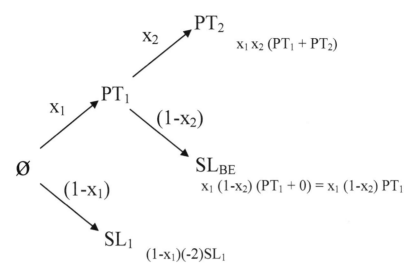

2-Tiered Strategy Directed Graph

strategy is used whereby the position is trailed with incremental stop-market orders. If the trader perceives a channeling or rotational market, he may choose to take a final exit at a pre-determined profit-target, for example at the outer edge of the trading channel. On the other hand, if the trader perceives a trending market, he may wish to use a trailing stop for the final exit. Some of the same techniques used to enter an e-mini trade are used to determine how to exit a winning trade.

The figure 2-Tiered Strategy Directed Graph, models the 2-tiered trade management strategy with a directed graph. As before, ø stands for the initial trade entry state. SL_1 is the first stop-loss state. PT_1 is the first profit-target state. SL_{BE} is a break even stop-loss state for the second half of the original $2x$ contracts. This is the state where the first profit-target was realized, stop-loss is moved to a break even level, but subsequently the trade does not realize the second profit-target and exits at the break even price for the remaining $1x$ contracts[4]. PT_2 is the second profit-target state. x_1 and x_2 are the probabilities of moving from ø to PT_1 and from PT_1 to PT_2.

---

[4] In the models here the SL_{BE} gives a modestly profitable trade.

Although the directed graph description makes no mention of trailing stop logic, the graph is sufficient to model either a second profit-target limit or the trailing stop-market strategy. This is because when modeling trade management some input value will be required to determine a final exit price. While the final exit price can be varied to analyze profit-loss scenarios, a final exit price is needed in order to "close" the directed graph. One means of modeling a trailing stop is to pick a percentage price reversal level from a final exit price and then use that value as a final exit profit-target. These considerations do not change the directed graph model.

Table Trade Management Strategy Profit and Loss 2 compares the basic unscaled strategy P&L with the 2-tiered strategy P&L. The basic strategy is labeled **1** and the 2-tiered **2**. The strategies share SL_1, PT_1 and x_1 values. The 2-tiererd strategy adds PT_2 and x_2 values to the table, with 12 ticks (=3 points) and 67%, respectively.

In addition, a column labeled "End-State %" calculates the probability of reaching the PT_2 profit-target. It is the product x_1 and x_2. While the individual probabilities of each new trade state in the graph are used to calculate expected value, it is helpful to keep various end-state probabilities in mind. In this case, with various intermediate probabilities, the overall probability of realizing a profit on both tiers of the 2-tiered strategy is 47%, or almost 50:50. This seems a reasonable figure.

Inputs		End-State %
1st P-T Win% (X1)	70%	
2nd P-T Win% (X2)	67%	0.47
1st P-T (PT1)	8	
2nd P-T (PT2)	12	
1st S-L Ticks (SL1)	8	
Strategies		

				P&L	
1	SL1	PT1	P&L	/CARS	
	-2.40	5.60	3.20	3.20	

					P&L	
2	SL1	SL-BE	PT2	P&L	/CARS	
	-4.80	1.85	9.38	6.43	3.21	

Trade Management Strategy Profit and Loss 2

The analysis of the basic and 2-tiered models, with the chosen inputs, shows that the 2-tiered model does not add value for the trader. But what we do have is a framework for analyzing strategies to see under what conditions a 2-tiered strategy might be preferred.

Three variants to the 2-tiered model that come to mind are:

1. Decreasing PT_1. We might take profits sooner in order to increase the probability of our reaching a no-lose position.
2. Increasing PT_2. We can investigate larger second contract profit-target, even making it a significant winning runner.
3. Consider $x_2 \geq x_1$. It may be correct to assume the probability of success decreases with each tier of a multi-tiered strategy. But what if, because of price momentum, we assume the chance of success improves if the initial tier of a trade is realized? This is modeled by considering $x_2 \geq x_1$ in the 2-tiered model.

Trade Management Strategy Profit and Loss 3 tests (1). PT_1 is lowered from eight to four ticks. PT_2 is correspondingly lowered by four ticks. Smaller PT values allow us to raise the x_1 and x_2 winning percentages. These modest changes significantly lower the basic unscaled P&L while improving, relative to the basic strategy, the 2-tiered result. This may be a preferred configuration for the 2-tiered strategy.

Trade Management Strategy Profit and Loss 4 tests (2). PT_2 is raised from 12 to 20 ticks (=5 points). An increased PT_2 value requires us to decrease the x_2 winning percentage. These modifications give equal basic unscaled and 2-tiered strategy results.

Trade Management Strategy Profit and Loss 5 tests (3). This is a more radical departure from our initial modeling. We make use of the End-State % calculation to ensure that our estimates of a best-case winning result are not over-stated. Here a 60% second contract winner may be reasonable. In this case we achieve a modest 24% improvement when using the 2-tiered model; probably not significant considering input variation.

We will return to the comparison of unscaled and 2-tiered models in a special section on scalping later in the chapter.

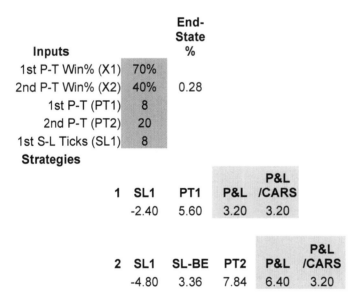

Inputs		End-State %
1st P-T Win% (X1)	75%	
2nd P-T Win% (X2)	70%	0.53
1st P-T (PT1)	4	
2nd P-T (PT2)	8	
1st S-L Ticks (SL1)	8	

Strategies

				P&L
1	SL1	PT1	P&L	/CARS
	-2.00	3.00	1.00	1.00

					P&L
2	SL1	SL-BE	PT2	P&L	/CARS
	-4.00	0.90	6.30	3.20	1.60

Trade Management Strategy Profit and Loss 3

Inputs		End-State %
1st P-T Win% (X1)	70%	
2nd P-T Win% (X2)	40%	0.28
1st P-T (PT1)	8	
2nd P-T (PT2)	20	
1st S-L Ticks (SL1)	8	

Strategies

				P&L
1	SL1	PT1	P&L	/CARS
	-2.40	5.60	3.20	3.20

					P&L
2	SL1	SL-BE	PT2	P&L	/CARS
	-4.80	3.36	7.84	6.40	3.20

Trade Management Strategy Profit and Loss 4

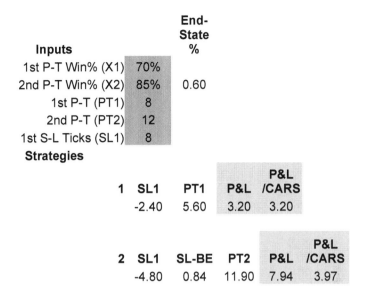

Inputs	End-State %
1st P-T Win% (X1)	70%
2nd P-T Win% (X2)	85%	0.60
1st P-T (PT1)	8
2nd P-T (PT2)	12
1st S-L Ticks (SL1)	8

Strategies

1	SL1	PT1	P&L	P&L /CARS
	-2.40	5.60	3.20	3.20

2	SL1	SL-BE	PT2	P&L	P&L /CARS
	-4.80	0.84	11.90	7.94	3.97

Trade Management Strategy Profit and Loss 5

3-Tiered Scale Strategy

A second popular scale-out strategy is referred to as the 3-tiered scale strategy. It takes off two tiers of contracts relatively quickly and retains a third tier for a longer-term winning runner.

Figure 3-Tiered Strategy Directed Graph is the directed graph model of the 3-tiered strategy. It is a direct extension of the 2-tiered case. There is one important addition to using the 3-tiered model. Because the final third of the original position is held for a long-term winning runner, PT_3, the third profit-target level used to estimate such a winning runner requires some attention.

The technique used relies again on the Average True Range (ATR) of the market to determine a reasonable winning runner price move. Based on the ATR data presented earlier, a reasonable long-term winning runner price move for the ES contract might be 10 points (40 ticks), representing approximately one to two hours of intra-day ES price action.

A winning runner probability must also be chosen (x_3). As with all model parameters, the trader can vary this input to reflect actual market conditions and to test profit-loss scenarios. In the studies here, an x_3 value which gives a 10-15% End-State% is used.

Table Trade Management Strategy Profit and Loss 6 gives a summary of 1- (**1**) (basic unscaled), 2- (**2**) and 3-tiered (**3**) strategy results with a single set of inputs.

The 3-tiered model offers a roughly 30% improvement over the 1- and 2-tier results (4.2/3.2). Based on this, it is believed to have merit, especially if the market develops an even larger winning runner for the final tier of contracts.

We can now investigate additional variations to the 2- and 3-tiered strategies.

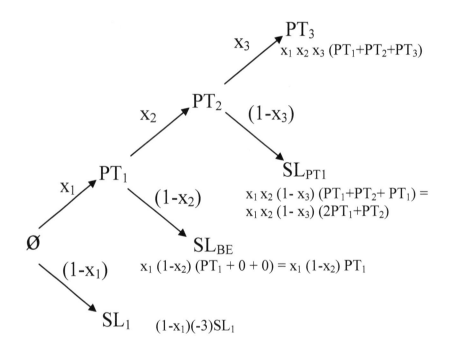

3-Tiered Strategy Directed Graph

Inputs		End-State %				
1st P-T Win% (X1)	70%					
2nd P-T Win% (X2)	67%	0.47				
Win. Runner% (X3)	33%	0.15				
1st P-T (PT1)	8					
2nd P-T (PT2)	12					
Win. Run. Ticks (PT3)	40					
1st S-L Ticks (SL1)	8					

Strategies

					P&L	
1	SL1	PT1	P&L	P&L /CARS		
	-2.40	5.60	3.20	3.20		

					P&L	
2	SL1	SL-BE	PT2	P&L	P&L /CARS	
	-4.80	1.85	9.38	6.43	3.21	

						P&L
3	SL1	SL-BE	SL-PT1	PT3	P&L	P&L /CARS
	-7.20	1.85	8.80	9.29	12.73	4.24

Trade Management Strategy Profit and Loss 6

Scratch Trades

Traders frequently describe scratching trades; that is, closing a position that does not quickly develop a profit for little or no loss. The models proposed already accommodate the scratch trade with the adjustment of model inputs.

For example, if the trader scratches 50% of his/her trades, and as a result claims a higher win/loss percentage in practice, model input parameter x_1 can be adjusted.

Doubling-Down

"Doubling-down," meaning to double one's original wager, is sometimes advocated by e-mini day-traders. As long as a stop-loss order is maintained to bound the maximum loss, it may make for a winning strategy[5].

The idea of doubling-down when trading the e-mini contract uses the following rationale and techniques:

- The trader perceives a price level where the market is expected to reverse. The price level may be based on support/resistance levels and other technical methods. The trader realizes it is impossible to precisely determine a reversal price so an averaging technique is used.
- A limit order is placed at an initial price level for half the total number of contracts the trader is willing to risk. At the time the position is opened, a maximum stop-loss market order is placed.
- If the market does reverse at the original estimated price level, fine – the trade is working on half the maximum number of contracts the trader might have used.
- If the market does not reverse at the original price level then a second limit order is used mid-way between the first entry point and the maximum stop-loss price. If executed it fills the second half of the allowed maximum number of contracts and the stop-loss market order quantity is doubled to the total number of open contracts.

---

[5] The Trade Examples chapter has additional material on the double-down.

The trader, knowing she cannot pin-point a reversal price, uses an averaging technique to enter the trade, while adhering to the discipline of a stop-loss should the entire trade fail.

The next chart shows a double-down trade setup in the making. The day's CTs were Unequivocally bearish so that short entries were attempted, and a short entry was conceived on retracement to a local maxima price level. But it was unclear at which recent local maxima the market might reverse. In this case, an initial entry at the closest local price maxima, minus two ticks, or 686.25 was attempted. If the market did not reverse from the 686-687 level, then a double-down entry was planned at the next most recent local maxima, minus two ticks, or 687.25. A final stop-loss value of 689 plus two ticks, or 689.50, was planned for the entire trade. The chart shows what in fact happened: The double-down entry was not executed as the first entry proved immediately profitable.

March 5, 2009. A Double-Down Trade. ES tick

The double-down strategy is modeled with the directed graph Double-Down Strategy Directed Graph. The model provides both scale-in and scale-out trade management. If the original position opens with 2x contracts and the double-down logic is not utilized a 2-tiered scale-out strategy is used. If a double-down position is taken then a total of 4x contracts are opened, and by removing 1x contracts at each profitable level (BE$_1$, PT$_{11}$, PT$_{21}$, PT$_3$), all contracts are eventually closed with 1x contracts remaining for a winning runner.   Obviously, the trade management techniques used in a double-down strategy have many variations.

While the double-down model adds complexity to the 2- and 3-tiered models, the directed graph organizes the analysis. Profit-loss formulas for the leaf nodes (trade exits) are easily constructed.   Using a spreadsheet with variable inputs makes re-calculation and analysis straightforward.

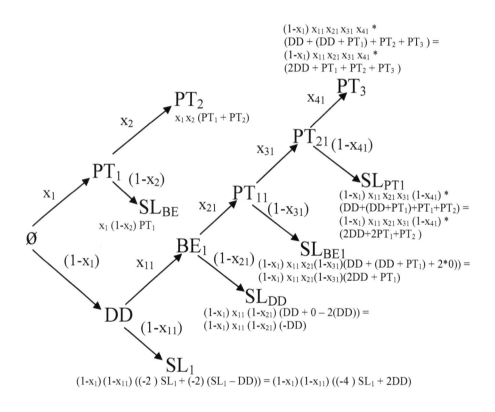

Double-Down Strategy Directed Graph

Table Trade Management Strategy Profit and Loss 7 (below) gives a profit-loss expected value calculation for the double-down, scale-in/scale-out strategy, labeled **D-D**. The P&L/CARS did not improve when moving from the 3-tiered to the Double Down Strategy.

Warrior Trading

Another form of doubling-down prevalent in the trading community has to do with aggressively adding contracts to a winning position when a longer-term trend can be identified. Many traders seek viable techniques for adding contracts to a winning position.

Rather than testing the market for a reversal, as described in the previous section, a warrior trade mentality adds contracts during price movement perceived to be developing into strong rallies or sell-offs. Price reversals or breakouts that occur at key support/resistance levels or with economic news that increases volatility may warrant more aggressive trading. Warrior trading describes aggressive trading that seeks to jump on a trend with additional contracts.

To study the effect of warrior trading, the directed graphs do not need to be modified but leaf node calculations are adjusted. Consider the 2-tiered strategy. Assume that as a result of realizing an initial profit-target (PT_2 in the modified Warrior Trading directed graph), and because of additional market conditions, it is determined that a strong trend is in-place and a warrior mentality is adopted. Additional contracts are added to the final profit-target (PT_W) and stop-loss break even (SL_{BE}) calculations; the probability x_W will reflect the chance of the warrior trend continuing.

The last entry in Table Trade Management Strategy Profit and Loss 7, labeled **W**, gives the profit-loss expected value calculation for a warrior model. A warrior contracts number has been added to account for additional contracts added at the PT_2 level. In this example, $2x$ warrior contracts are added.

The Warrior Trading strategy gives a huge increase in P&L/CARS, almost four times the 1-tiered basic baseline strategy. There is significant hearsay in the futures trading community about warrior trading being necessary for significant day-trading profitability. The model results are consistent with this. However, warrior trading may simply beg the larger question of how to trade. Namely, if warrior trades were readily discernable, they would be the trading method of choice. But warrior trading can lead to repeated losses that cause traders to look for lower-risk, more predictable strategies.

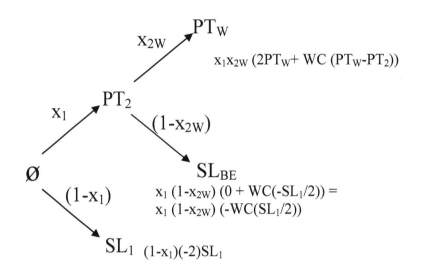

Warrior 2-Tiered Strategy Directed Graph

Inputs		End-State %
1st P-T Win% (X1)	70%	
2nd P-T Win% (X2)	67%	0.47
Win. Runner% (X3)	33%	0.15
1st P-T (PT1)	8	
2nd P-T (PT2)	12	
Win. Run. Ticks (PT3)	40	
1st S-L Ticks (SL1)	8	
D-D Ticks (DD)	4	
X11 %	66%	0.46
X21 %	80%	0.37
X31 %	80%	0.30
X41 %	60%	0.18
Warrior CARS (WC)	2	
Warrior Win% (X2W)	75%	0.35
Warrior Ticks (PT2W)	32	

Strategies

1	SL1	PT1	P&L	P&L /CARS
	-2.40	5.60	3.20	3.20

2	SL1	SL-BE	PT2	P&L	P&L /CARS
	-4.80	1.85	9.38	6.43	3.21

3	SL1	SL-BE	SL-PT1	PT3	P&L	P&L /CARS
	-7.20	1.85	8.80	9.29	12.73	4.24

D-D	SL-BE	PT2	SL1	SL-DD	SL-BE1	SL-PT1	PT3	P&L	P&L /CARS
	1.85	9.38	-2.45	-0.16	0.51	1.82	5.17	16.12	4.03

W	SL1	SL-BE	PT2	P&L	P&L /CARS
	-4.80	-1.40	54.60	48.40	12.10

Trade Management Strategy Profit and Loss 7

Scalping

There is a good amount of debate among day-traders regarding the pros and cons of scalping versus swing trading (achieving winning runners). We can use the basic unscaled strategy to further investigate scalping. To make the discussion tractable, we will again compare the unscaled strategy against the 2-tiered. Previously, we determined that the 2-tiered model gave improved results, relative to the basic strategy, when fast profit-taking was used on the first set of contracts.

If we assume aggressive scalping, we might use a 4-tick profit-target and a 4-6 tick stop-loss. Assume a 5-tick stop-loss. A 70% x_1 winning percentage can model successful scalping. The 2-tiered strategy will use the same values for PT_1 and SL_1, and a conservative second tier profit-target of six ticks. A 67% x_2 winning percentage models a successful trader who achieves a second profit-target on 47% of his or her trades. We get the following result from the directed graph analysis:

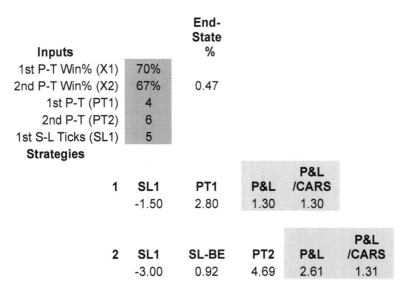

Inputs		End-State %		
1st P-T Win% (X1)	70%			
2nd P-T Win% (X2)	67%	0.47		
1st P-T (PT1)	4			
2nd P-T (PT2)	6			
1st S-L Ticks (SL1)	5			
Strategies				
				P&L
1	SL1	PT1	P&L	**/CARS**
	-1.50	2.80	1.30	1.30
				P&L
2	SL1	SL-BE	PT2	P&L	**/CARS**
	-3.00	0.92	4.69	2.61	1.31

Trade Management Strategy Profit and Loss 8: Scalping Vs. 2-Tiered

The result is that there is no difference between the unscaled scalping strategy and the 2-tiered strategy; that is, there is no benefit to trading more than the scalp.

We make an adjustment to the scalping analysis. By increasing the second tier profit-target to something more than twice the scalp value, while decreasing the second tier winning percentage consistently, we generate a 2-tiered strategy that is a marked improvement to the scalping (a 70% improvement in profitability). From this we conclude that when it comes to scalping:

1. Scalping can be as profitable as a 2-tiered strategy when the 2-tiered second profit-target is not significantly larger than the scalp.
2. A 2-tiered strategy can be a significant improvement (>50%) if the second profit-target is on the order of 2.5-3 times the scalp profit-target.

Again, as with all the strategy analyses, these are rules-of-thumb and depend on the inputs; in particular the close relationship between stop-loss, profit-target and winning percentages. The importance of the directed graph analysis is not any one result, but the ability if gives the trader to experiment with strategies in order to gain an understanding of their relative merit.

Inputs		End-State %			
1st P-T Win% (X1)	70%				
2nd P-T Win% (X2)	55%	0.39			
1st P-T (PT1)	4				
2nd P-T (PT2)	12				
1st S-L Ticks (SL1)	5				
Strategies					
					P&L
1	SL1	PT1	P&L	/CARS	
	-1.50	2.80	1.30	1.30	
					P&L
2	SL1	SL-BE	PT2	P&L	/CARS
	-3.00	1.26	6.16	4.42	2.21

Trade Management Strategy Profit and Loss 9: Scalping Vs. 2-Tiered (2)

Limit and Stop Market Trade Entry Comparison

In this section we analyze the expected value results of Limit order versus Stop Market order entry.

Consider the following price pattern, the BOP SHORT:

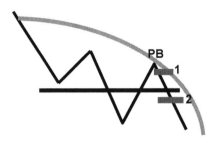

Two entries are defined, a Limit order from the 20-EMA (1) and a Stop Market order from the second breakout (2). Some traders prefer (1) because they are getting a better entry price. Some traders prefer (2) because they want to enter the market when it is moving in the direction of their trade.

In the case of (1), initial stop-loss will be set just outside of the EMA line or the most recent swing high. In the case of (2), initial stop-loss will be set just above the recent swing high (setting it just above the breakout level is often too tight). Entry 2 requires a wider initial stop-loss. This is shown in the price chart from February 10, 2010, below. The trader makes use of the most recent swing high (PB) plus a few ticks as the initial stop-loss level. In the trade from February 10, that is 1060.50; and 1060.50 makes a good value as it is two ticks above a fairly BN of 1060.

February 10, 2009. BOP SHORT. ES 764-tick

The Limit order (1) enters at the 1059.75, just below the 20-EMA. In this case, a three tick stop-loss is required (1060.50 – 1059.75). The Stop Market order (2) enters at 1058.75, one tick below the breakout level (1059.00). In this case, a seven tick stop-loss is required (1060.50 - 1058.75).

For the purposes of a rudimentary analysis, we can assume the following stop-loss levels for the Limit and Stop Market entries:

- Limit order: 4 ticks
- Stop Market order: 8 ticks

To keep the analysis simple, we will consider the unscaled strategy with a six tick profit-target for both cases. What remains is to determine the winning percentages for the two cases.

It can be argued that the Stop Market case should be given a lower winning percentage because it requires price move in our direction a larger amount beginning from the EMA line. Or, it can be argued that if the market is entered with the Stop Market order, then it has shown its hand and we can use a higher winning percentage in this case. Rather than address the issue right off, we will fix the winning percentage for both entries at a somewhat conservative 67% to first get an idea of the the merits, if any, of entering earlier (the Limit order case).

Table Trade Management Strategy Profit and Loss 10: Limit vs. Stop Market (1) shows the Limit order entry as almost twice as profitable.

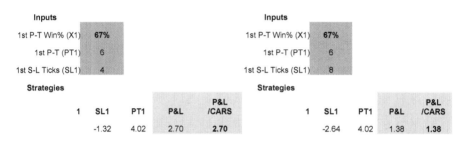

Trade Management Strategy Profit and Loss 10: Limit vs. Stop Market (1)

Next, we adjust the winning percentage of the Stop Market entry to see what increase in winning percentage is needed to equal the Limit order entry. Table Trade Management Strategy Profit and Loss 11: Limit vs. Stop Market (2) shows that the Stop Market winning percentage must be increased from 67% to 77% in order to equal the Limit order entry.

The reader can draw his or her own conclusions as to whether the technique of entering the market only when it moves in the direction of the trade is warranted, if a 15% relative winning percentage increase is required (77-67)/67. When the trader is confident in the trade, with other indications pointing to a successful position, then the Limit order entry may be preferred.

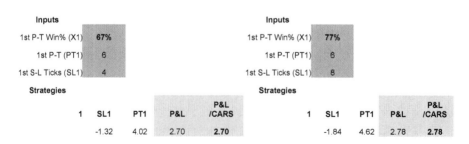

Trade Management Strategy Profit and Loss 11: Limit vs. Stop Market (2)

Strategy Analysis and Conclusions

The model outputs are highly dependent on their inputs ("garbage in/garbage out"). However, by holding inputs constant it is possible to reach general conclusions that can help the trader. Win-Loss% inputs will be the most difficult values on which to agree, and there is an obvious and direct correlation among the Win-Loss% and stop-loss and profit-target parameters. The models can easily be tested across a range of values to give the trader information.

Conclusions from the model experiments are:
- The basic unscaled 1-tiered strategy is compelling based on its simplicity and relative profitability. However, it does not let the trader participate in winning runners.
- The 2-tiered strategy does not add significantly to the 1-tiered strategy unless a fast 1st tier profit-target is used – scalping the first set of contracts – or the second profit-target is 2.5-3X the unscaled 1st tier profit-target – significantly swinging the 2nd tier.
- The 3-tiered strategy may offer an approximate 30% improvement over the 2-tiered strategy.
- The double-down strategy improves the 2-tiered strategy slightly but less than that offered by the 3-tiered strategy.
- The warrior strategy offers the most significant return but may simply beg the question; that is, it assumes an aggressive trade entry setup that has not actually been defined. Warrior trading may simply fall prey to chasing.

Based on the strategy modeling:
1. The 1-tiered strategy is a viable scalping strategy, relative to the 2-tiered strategy.
2. The 2-tiered strategy should use fast 1st tier profit-taking with a 2nd tier profit-target that is roughly 2-3X above a 1-tiered scalping strategy. That is, scalp then swing with some conviction.
3. The 3-tiered strategy may be a modest improvement over the 2-tiered for the purposes of swing trading winning runners.
4. Warrior trading cannot be recommended because setup rules have not been clearly defined. But warrior trading again points to the importance of establishing winning runner positions.
5. When the trader perceives a trending market (Unequivocal CTs), he should attempt to stay with a winning runner position. Three minute charts that seek to keep the trader in the market can be used in these situations.

The next section, Achieving Winning Runners, describes how to maintain contracts open to capture winning runners. Following that, the section Trade Management Mechanics covers details of trade order entry and exit.

Achieving Winning Runners

While the press may report a modest change in the stock market for the day, leaving the impression with the public that the day's trading was predictable or methodical, day-traders know how volatile a trading session can be. Even if the S&P 500 closed up or down just a few points, the day-trading participant may experience a market that moved back and forth through 20, 30, 40 or more index points. It is intra-day volatility that makes the day-trading endeavor compelling.

Given the daily volatility of the stock market, and hence the stock index futures, intra-day reversals are all too common. Even the experienced trader is constantly having to push himself not to take quick profits, afraid that if he doesn't he'll lose everything he's gained or, even worse, go deeper in the hole for the day. One of the most difficult trading disciplines to master is the ability to retain winning runners.

Martin "Buzzy" Schwartz, considered one or the finest stock index futures traders, and author of the entertaining and highly informative trading book, Pit Bull, HarperCollins Publishers, 1998, states one of his nagging problems was taking profits too quickly – and Schwartz is a pre-eminent trader. When I take a profit quickly, only to see how much I might have made if I'd exercised more patience, I think back to Schwartz's book.

It is important to get a trade quickly to a position of low- or no-risk in order to participate in winning runners. Expert e-mini scalpers who read this may think otherwise, and I admit I enjoy scalping profits. But scalping day after day costs a lot, in physical energy and commissions. Perhaps the ideal day-trading regime incorporates a middle-ground between scalping and longer-term winners. At times the market may dictate both approaches. But in general, finding a means of capturing moderate or longer-term trends as they occur during the day remains an important goal.

I am convinced that the only way to establish winning runners is with automation. Essentially, we can't expect to overcome the overwhelming desire to book profits without help.

For most of the last 10 years, our family owned a beautiful golden retriever. While still a puppy, we took Chumba to obedience training at the local county fairgrounds. The instructors were knowledgeable dog owners and trainers with many years of experience training all kinds of dogs. I remember one evening an instructor spoke to me about golden retrievers. She said, No matter how well trained, if off the leash and a small animal runs in front of your dog, he's going to chase it. There's nothing you can do about it. It's just part of the dog that will never go away.

Day-traders and profits are like Chumba and our neighborhood's cats and squirrels. We can talk all we want about the importance of trading with the trend and achieving winning runners, but it seems that without some external, automatic mechanism as a guide (our leash?), we just can't not take certain profits. Perhaps what's important is to recognize this fact and then find the right tools to deal with it.

There are two parts to the automation used by the e-mini stock index futures system to retain winning runner contracts. First, the system needs a scale-out strategy that gets the trade to a low- or no-risk winning runner position. That is why measuring scale-out strategies was important. Second, the trader needs a means of automatically trailing stops in order to stay in a trade. Having an automated trailing stops technique is the key because it unambiguously defines how to stay in a trade.

The downside to automated trailing stops is that traders often experience stopped trades with little better results than if they had scalped and taken quick profits. Trades move back to the trailing stop-loss point and exit near where the trader first wanted to take profits. This is similar to relying entirely on moving averages to trade. At first it looks like moving average cross-over works, but in practice there are repeated whipsaws and one becomes disenchanted with them. We will address this issue as part of the system's trailing stop automation. In fact, while arguing for strict automation, we will see a hybrid approach used with trailing stops which strikes a balance between 100% automation and the goal of eliminating an inefficient use of stop-loss.

An initial automated trailing stop system can be based on the J. Welles Wilder, Jr., "Parabolic Stop and Reverse" (SAR) indicator. Wilder was a creative developer of technical indicators, including the widely used RSI (Relative Strength Index). See the excellent text, Trading Systems and Methods, Perry J. Kaufman, John Wiley & Sons, for an in-depth description of the Parabolic SAR, RSI and other technical indicators.

The Parabolic SAR trails a market with an exponentially smoothed price that can be used for setting trailing stops. See the following chart from March 6th. Parabolic SAR can be used to set trailing stops but it requires an almost continuous update of the stop-loss price. Furthermore, it does not comprehend rapid price moves because of the nature of its price smoothing.

An improved means of automatically generating trailing stop prices has been developed by Teresa Lo, a professional trader and the founder of InVivo Analytics. InVivo.Stops is not simply price smoothing some distance from recent lows or highs but an algorithm incorporating key price level changes and price ledges above and below the market where stop-loss is effective. An example of InVivo.Stops is shown next. (See the book's appendices for a Web reference to InVivo Analytics. TradeStation and eSignal indicators are available for the InVivo.Stops.)

Because Invivo.Stops provide intelligent stops and do not require a continuous update of the trailing stop price, they are an excellent tool for automating trailing stops. The Trade Management Mechanics section describes how the NinjaTrader platform is used for trade order entry and management. Invivo.Stops are easily updated using NinjaTrader so that a trade can be automatically and mechanically trailed with stops, once NinjaTrader executes a profit-target on a fast-exit first tier set of contracts.

One can intervene in the use of automatic trailing stops in two cases. First, a trade will sometimes be manually closed ahead of automated stop-loss. This is shown in the next chart, also from March 6, 2009. A MACD-Price Divergence short trade is depicted with a limit order at the 20-EMA retracement. Shortly thereafter, the trade is exited with a limit order that over-rides the trailing stop market order. This result is a winning trade of 3.5 points, a two point improvement over the trailing stop.

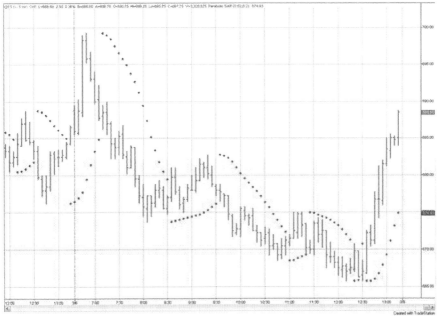

March 6, 2009. Parabolic SAR for Trailing Stops. ES 5-min

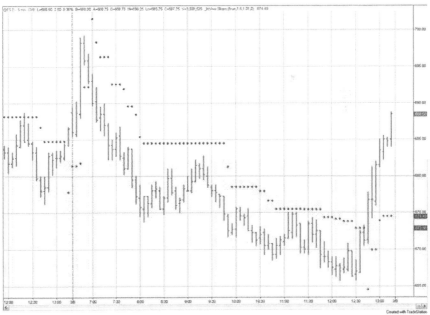

March 6, 2009. Invivo.Stops for Trailing Stops. ES 5-min

The reader will most likely become exasperated at this point, thinking: You're breaking the rules you just prescribed! This is a fair assessment. However, the trade was initially managed using automated stop-loss and the use of automation took the trade to a reasonable winner that might not have been possible if a scalping mentality prevailed. What changed was an MACD rotation from overbought to oversold and this was followed by an MACD-Price Divergence in the opposing direction[6]. Because of this the trade was closed prior to automated stop-loss. Again, we made sure the automated trailing stop logic initially kicked-in, but when there was good reason to over-ride it, we did so.

The system is discretionary and trading is not a science. It is the introduction of trailing stop automation that is important, not its blind use.

On the other hand, it is often clear when over-riding automated trailing stops is a mistake. In the following chart from January 8, 2009, a MACD-Price Divergence trade quickly moves to a break even position. It is a mistake to exit the trade with the MACD still well above the Oversold level. In this case, all the trader's ducks are in-line and it's best to simply follow the trailing stops; at least until an MACD Oversold condition occurs.

The second case of automated trailing stop intervention occurs in the other direction: Stop prices are moved farther away from the market than those generated by the software. The next example is such a case. On March 2, 2009, the CTs were Unequivocally bearish. It appeared another strong Trend Day down was unfolding, part of the continued 2008-09 bear market. This is a case where we take a more aggressive tack with the position (a warrior mentality?) and look to stay with the trade.

The chart from March 2nd shows definite Unequivocal CTs. Here the goal was to short the market and follow the trend for a good part of the day. Because of the Trend Day determination an ES 3-minute chart was used. A narrow IB indicated an IBL Range Extension possibility.

---

[6] One could argue the trade should have been reversed at this point, short to long. I do not practice trade reversals.

March 6, 2009. Manual Exit via MACD. ES tick

January 8, 2009. Stay in the Trade with Trailing Stops. NQ tick

Entry was made when the market retraced to the IBL, which corresponded to a 3-minute 20-EMA retracement. In the management of this trade, one ES point was added to all the InVivo.Stops – we did not want to get stopped out early by a local retracement. Automated trailing stops were used, but they were adjusted based on the day-type. The trade was eventually stopped out for a nine point winner.

In the next section, all the Trade Management components described so far are put together. What may at this point appear to be overly complicated trade execution environment will be turned into a few mouse clicks using software automation.

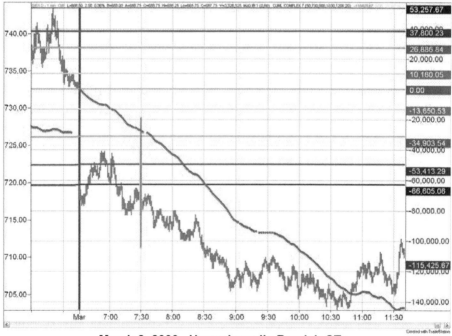

March 2, 2009. Unequivocally Bearish CTs

March 2, 2009. Stop Prices Raised. ES 3-min

Trade Management Mechanics

The e-mini stock index futures system uses the TradeStation desktop for charting and indicator execution to identify trade setups. NinjaTrader[7] software is used for order entry and trade management strategy execution. NinjaTrader provides an easy-to-use front-end for defining trade strategies and it is a reliable and efficient order execution platform.

It is easy to define multi-tiered trade strategies with NinjaTrader and NinjaTrader run-time support automatically adjusts positions based on order execution. For example, if a trade is specified to open with three contracts and stop-loss is specified for all contracts, then when the three contracts initially fill there will be a three contract stop-loss order entered automatically. If a first-tier contract is filled on a fast-exit profit-target, then NinjaTrader automatically adjusts the stop-loss order, decrementing

---

[7] It should also be mentioned that NinjaTrader supports its own charting and indicator suite as part of a complete trading desktop solution. See the Appendices for a Web reference to NinjaTrader.

the number of stop-loss contracts by one. Specifying this type of automatic execution is very easy with the NinjaTrader interface[8].

The graphic on the following page, NinjaTrader – Strategy Definition, shows the NinjaTrader price ladder and strategy parameter interface. A pre-programmed strategy named "ES Basic 2x3" matches the 3-Tiered strategy described earlier. We see an order quantity of '3'; for the 3-Tiered strategy, this can be a 3x multiple. The '3 Target' radio button is selected and a strategy action for each of the three tiers is defined as:

	1 Target	2 Target	3 Target
Qty:	1	1	1
Stop loss:	10	10	10
Profit target:	4	6	0

This closely matches the parameters of the 3-tiered strategy model. Notice that the '3 Target' column specifies a Profit target of 0, which is the winning runner contract that will be managed with trailing stops.

A right mouse click over the ATM Strategy field (ES Basic 2x3) brings up a simple dialog box in order to save the named strategy and make it available at run-time for use with a new order.

At the time of order entry, the ATM Strategy drop-down menu allows the selection of the strategy the trader wishes to run (ES Basic 1x2 – the 2-tiered strategy; ES Basic 2x3 – the 3-tiered strategy; etc.). This is shown in the second NinjaTrader price ladder graphic titled NinjaTrader – Selecting a User-Defined Strategy for Order Entry.

Once the trade is open, should the first two tiers be reached, then Invivo.Stops are updated in NinjaTrader via its Basic Entry interface. As the trailing stop prices are incremented (decremented) one simply clicks the Basic Entry order item to adjust a trailing stop price[9].

---

[8] NinjaTrader will support much more sophisticated strategies than the 2- and 3-tiered models defined here. In fact, the trade management strategies used in this book only scratch the surface of NinjaTrader capabilities. The reader is urged to investigate the additional features in the NinjaTrader product.
[9] A more elegant adjustment of price uses the original order entry price ladder and the mouse to simply drag the order to the new desired price. I have found mouse click fumbles make it more reliable to manually click an existing order to a new price. Perhaps I'm just getting old.

BUY	PRICE	SELL
	690.50	
	690.25	
	690.00	9
	689.75	253
	689.50	5
	689.25	2
	689.00	3
	688.75	
	(2) 688.50	
	688.25	
	688.00	
	687.75	
	687.50	
	687.25	
	687.00	
	686.75	
	686.50	
27	**686.25**	
87	686.00	
76	685.75	
76	685.50	
75	685.25	
	685.00	
MARKET	PnL	MARKET

| < | REV | FLAT | CLOSE | C |

Instrument:	ES 03-09 ⌄	Order qty:	3 ⌄
Account:	⌄	TIF:	Day ⌄
ATM Strategy:	ES Basic 2x3		⌄

ATM Strategy parameters (ticks)

	◯ 1 Target	◯ 2 Target	◉ 3 Target
Qty:	1 ⌄	1 ⌄	1 ⌄
Stop loss:	10 ⌄	10 ⌄	10 ⌄
Profit target:	4 ⌄	6 ⌄	0 ⌄
Stop strategy:	<None> ⌄	<None> ⌄	<None> ⌄

NinjaTrader – Strategy Definition

NinjaTrader – Selecting a User-Defined Strategy for Order Entry

The Basic Entry interface is shown in the third NinjaTrader graphic, NinjaTrader – Basic Order Entry Trailing Stop Adjustment. A Buy Stop stop-loss order has been entered by the NinjaTrader strategy software at a price of 687.00. If the Invivo.Stops indicate a new stop-loss price of 686.00, then the decrement price button is clicked four times (4 ticks) to automatically move the trailing stop to the new level.

A new trade is initiated by:

1. Selecting the contract (ES, TF, NQ, YM);
2. Selecting the strategy (2-tiered, 3-tiered, etc.);
3. Clicking on the limit price (Buy or Sell) on the price ladder[10].

Clicking a limit price on the price ladder initiates the selected strategy and NinjaTrader enters the initial limit order for the strategy. If the entry limit order is filled, NinjaTrader will automatically enter stop-loss market and profit-target limit orders. The trader might adjust the stop-loss orders up or down based on current market conditions using the NinjaTrader Basic Entry interface. If a double-down strategy is used, the trader will enter a second limit order using the price ladder and the identical strategy. Final stop-loss for the original and the double-down entry can by synchronized using the Basic Entry interface.

If the first tier profit-target limit order is filled, NinjaTrader automatically decrements the stop-loss market order. This is repeated for the second tier as well. In the case of the 2-tiered strategy, the final stop-loss order is automatically cancelled and the trader is flat.

In the case of the 3-tiered strategy, if the second tier is profitably closed, the final stop-loss order represents a break even trade. It can be moved closer to the entry price if the trader wishes to lock in some profit[11]. Stop-loss orders are adjusted using the NinjaTrader Basic Entry interface. From this point forward there is not an outstanding profit-target limit order for the final contract. Invivo.Stops can be used to repeatedly adjust the

---

[10] NinjaTrader has a somewhat awkward interface for entering Stop Market orders on the SuperDOM. CTRL+Mouse-wheel-tap are used with the mouse over the price ladder.

[11] The strategies used at the beginning of the chapter are a few examples of many viable stop-loss and profit-target strategies. The reader is encouraged to develop additional strategies and strategy stop-loss and profit-target parameters that match his or her trading goals and psychology. See the Appendices for a Web reference to the profit and loss spreadsheet.

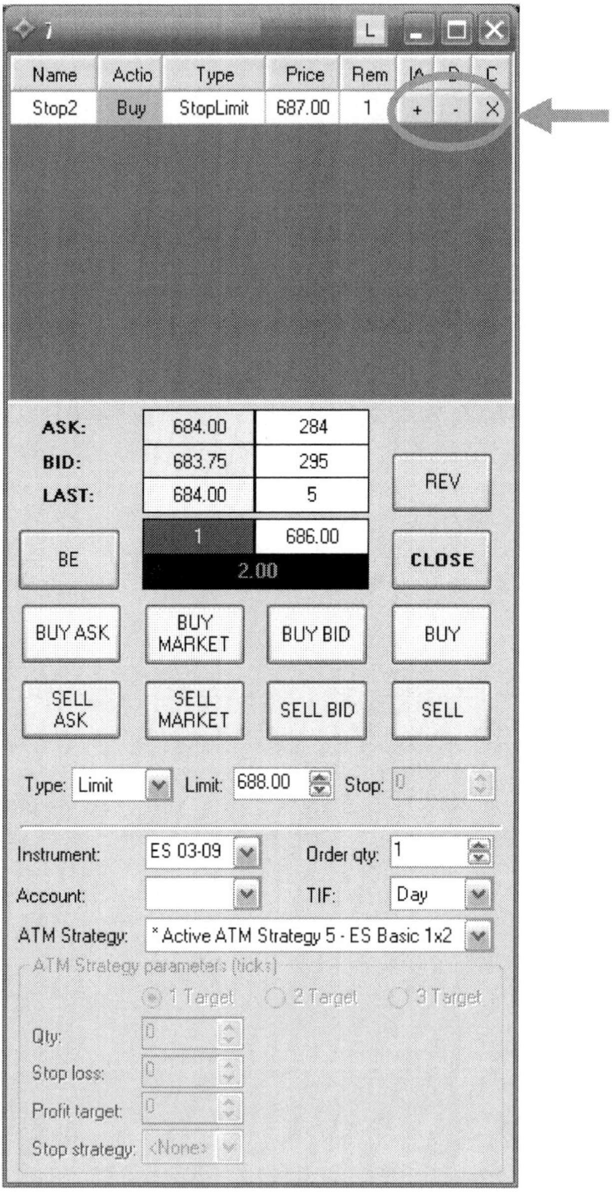

NinjaTrader – Basic Order Entry Trailing Stop Adjustment

stop-loss order on third tier contracts, or the trader may wish to prematurely close the entire position using a new profit-target limit order, which can be entered using either the NinjaTrader price ladder or the Basic Entry interface.

Because many of the e-mini stock index futures setups are reversal trades, it is imperative that NinjaTrader strategies (or equivalent software) are used to initiate and manage positions. Often, key price levels give enough immediate retracement to realize the first or second tier profit targets and place the trader in a break even position, ready for a possible winning runner. But without automation, fast-exit profit-targets are easily missed and, even more importantly, automated stop-loss protects the trader against sudden adverse moves in the market.

The next chart, January 23, 2009, shows a trade which was just average in its profitability but was well executed and makes a good example. Here, the Day's Previous High (DPH) was tested. A 3-tiered strategy resting limit order was placed at DPH minus two ticks, or 831.75. Once filled the market moved to 832.50, well within the 8-10 tick stop-loss range used in the 3-tiered strategy definition, and then began to move lower. Profits at 830.75 and 830.25 were automatically taken and the trailing stop was moved to the entry price, 831.75. This was adjusted twice, down to 830.50 at its lowest level. The market stopped selling, began to move higher and the trade was stopped out with an 830.50 trailing stop. The trade returned a total of 4 + 6 + 5 = 15 ticks. No sizeable winning runner, but a respectable result.

The example illustrates the way in which automation is used to fade the market and keep the trader profitable. Importantly, the market was not chased from the DPH price, but a limit order anticipated price action. This is crucial. NinjaTrader automated strategy execution supports this type of trading. If the market had been chased in this case, it is likely a losing trade would have resulted.

The next chapter, Trade Examples, will offer additional example trades using the setups and management of the e-mini stock index futures system.

January 23, 2009. A Small Winner.   ES tick

§§§

Trade Examples, Do's and Don'ts, Psychology

A few years ago, Ravi, a very good friend and business partner, and I decided to conduct a trading experiment – something along the lines of the Turtle Traders experiment run by the famous commodity traders Richard Dennis and William Eckhardt, although on a much smaller scale, of course.

Dennis and Eckhardt had long discussed the issue of whether traders were born with the skill and temperament necessary to be successful or whether trading could be taught to anyone with a quick mind and willingness to learn. This was another case of the age-old nature/nurture argument regarding human behavior. Dennis, on a trip to Asia, came across a tub of baby turtles and he imagined turning, with the proper training, a group of new initiates into traders. Thus the term Turtle Traders came to be. Eckhardt was less sure trading could be taught.

Dennis and Eckhardt advertised for trainees and from hundreds of highly qualified candidates (who wouldn't want the chance to be instructed by the legendary traders?) selected a few dozen for several weeks of training, after which they were given individual accounts to trade. Turtle trading rules were well-defined and to be followed carefully. If the rules were broken, then the trader was dismissed from the experiment. The program turned out a number of profitable traders. To this day, one can find a large amount of material in the media and on the Web about the Turtle Traders and Turtle Trading techniques[1]. The Turtle Trading story has become part of the folk-lore of the contemporary trading community.

Ravi has a nephew, Vivek, who recently graduated with a degree in engineering. Vivek was helping us develop analytical tools for the SP options selling program we were running. It was immediately clear from working with Vivek that he was bright and a quick study.

---

[1] Later Dennis and Eckhardt apparently stated that the original Turtle Trader methods became obsolete or at least in need of updating to current market conditions. Originally, the Turtle Traders agreed to a non-disclosure agreement. A desire to profit from the Turtle Trading legacy overshadowed the secrecy agreement or, with the passing of time, the trading secrets became less relevant and were publicized.

During the summer when Vivek was not in school, Ravi opened a $10,000 TradeStation account and I began to teach Vivek what I knew of day-trading the e-mini stock index futures. Initially, Vivek said he would be happy to net, after commissions, $100 per day.

After watching my trading for a couple of weeks Vivek began to trade on his own. (This was before the advent of the current generation of trade simulators, which direct access brokers have recently incorporated in real-time day-trading desktops. We would have first made use of a simulator if one had been available.) While Vivek had a number of winning days, netting profits in excess of a several hundred dollars, he quickly ran the account down to $7500 and it was decided to end the experiment.

There was an important result that came from our small trading experiment and something I still recall regularly to this day. It was something Vivek said near the end of it:

> *I know I don't have the techniques needed to be profitable at this, but I do know that it requires <u>anticipation</u> to be successful.*

In that one statement, Vivek captured an important kernel of what is needed to day-trade, and his words are worth every penny of the $2500 lost in the experiment. Vivek's idea can't be over-stated: To win at day-trading, one has to *anticipate* the market. The e-mini stock index futures system in this book is based on anticipating the market.

It can take several years to fully comprehend, and put into practice, anticipation in one's trading. Overcoming the psychological aspects of trading can be the most difficult aspect to realizing profitability. Until one has learned to stop chasing, getting "short-in-the-hole," making up chart patterns that seemingly must be traded, trading at the wrong time of day, shorting rallies early, and other similar errors, it is not possible to make money.

Anticipating the market rather than chasing it means using orders set ahead of the market (Limit or Stop Market) to open positions, and at prices that are predefined by the day's architecture of price action. Orders can be based on a price pattern and absolute price level (IBH/L, DPH/L, PDH/L, Pivot, Open, S1/2, R1/2) or a relative price retracement (3-minute and tick chart 20-EMA retracement). Whatever price level determination is used, one simply cannot enter positions with market orders that chase.

Initially my trading did not anticipate the market. Perhaps the only thing I did correctly was to trade small and use stop-loss discipline. At least with these two techniques I was able to make the many hundreds, even thousands, of trades needed to learn.

At first, trade-small and always with stop-loss discipline. The goal is to maintain an account that allows one to gain the necessary experience. The new trade simulators available today are a great way to begin practicing, even as paper-trading has none of the emotion of real account trading.

This chapter gives a number of trading examples, do's and don'ts, and thoughts on trade psychology. The examples reinforce the trade setups and management techniques described in the previous chapters of the book, and there are some useful rules-of-thumb that add to the trading system.

§§§

Trade Management Automation

Automated trade management, as described in the previous chapter, has the benefit of relieving the trader from many of the headaches of correctly handling an open position. Furthermore, when scaled trade management is combined with automated trailing stop logic, the trader is more likely to achieve low risk winning runners.

A benefit of automation is its accuracy. When breakouts and reversals are used for trade setups it is often the case that immediate price action will move the trade to a first-tier, fast profit number of ticks, and from there the trade may be configured to a no-lose, on-the-house position. Automation can give the trader more confidence in setting orders ahead of the market because it is able to quickly and accurately take off initial fast exit contracts while protecting a trade with initial stop-loss orders. One of the goals of the e-mini stock index futures trading system is to get the trader into as many no-lose, on-the-house trades as possible so that potential winning runners can be achieved with little risk.

The chart from February 25, 2009, is an example of a trade which, while not making a significant profit, is considered a successful use of the e-mini system. Here, a short from the Day's Previous High (DPH) is attempted late in the day (12:23pm Pacific). MACD OB and the DPH coincide to substantiate the entry. A three-tiered strategy is used and NinjaTrader automation is able to execute fast-exit profit targets of four and six ticks. Because of the day's volatility, it is decided to move final stop-loss to just two ticks above the entry price. Some six minutes after the initial position is taken, the final tier of contracts is closed based on the stop loss (again, automatically by NinjaTrader) for a profit of 4 + 6 - 2 = 8 ticks or two ES points. Some traders consider taking two points from the ES contract a good result.

While this trade was not held for a large winner, it is a good example of what the trader will often experience when carefully setting entries at price levels and employing trade management automation. Discretionary trading is part science and part art, and price action is never repeated exactly. Software automation helps the trader manage market volatility.

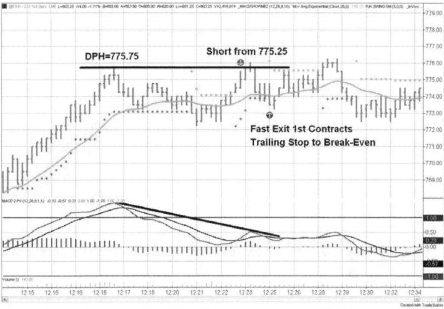

February 25, 2009. Trade Automation. ES tick

The Importance of Failures and Information from Failures

The trader should be on his or her toes when a trading rule or expected price pattern fails and realize there may be useful and tradable information from the failure. Third-Time-Up/Down offers a good example of this. What if the market fails on the third-time-up/down? There is good information from that. Specifically we would expect price to reverse from the local resistance/support area.

The March 27, 2009 chart shows a failed third-time-up. Sure enough, the market retreated with the failure. The trade in this case would have been a predefined short from the DPH using the PDT SHORT (Price Level plus Double Top) or 3TF SHORT (Third Time Failure). Note that flat and Equivocal CTs supported a short from the DPH price level.

March 27, 2009. Third-time-up Failure. PDT or 3TF SHORT. ES 3-min

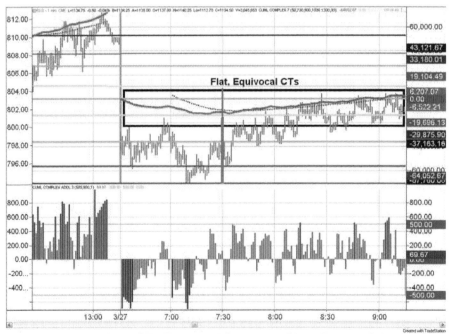

March 27, 2009. CTs Equivocal Support a Short Fade. ES 3-min

The February 17, 2010 chart, below, shows a failed third-time-down[2]. When reviewing this price action, one wonders if it was even possible to avoid or whether it represents the inherent uncertainty of trading.

The chart's price action shows a series of lower highs (3) above a well-defined support level at the 1090 price, perhaps a BN. A third time pushdown seems a logical place for a Sell Stop Market order, with a price of 1090 minus one or two ticks. A Sell Stop at 1089.75 would have filled and then turned immediately into a loser. No system can deliver 100% of the time; perhaps this was a losing trade that had to be experienced.

However, in this case, a review of the CTs showed that short positions were risky given almost no selling up to the time of the expected breakout. In addition, the 20-EMA was not convincingly bearish but had a meandering form to it – the 3TD price pattern is most effective when the 20-EMA shows a significant negative slope, indicating a strong descending triangle pattern.

In any case, once the failure to move lower occurred, the market proceeded higher in the reverse direction. Some traders might have quickly reversed a short position. Other traders would have waited, viewing the beginnings of the failure as a breakout pullback, and even something to be shorted again (the BOP SHORT pattern). The chart points out the difficulty of trying to predict the market.

Failure of an expected event can give the trader useful and tradable information. Examples of failures, and how they can be traded, include:

- Failed third time up/down often leads to a reversal.
- IBH/L RE failure implies rotation back into the IB.
- VAH/L rejection implies rotation back into the VA (the 80% Rule).
- Price that holds within the PDH/L by one or two points (ES contract) implies rotation may occur; e.g., a Neutral Day.
- Price that holds repeatedly at the DPH/L may result in a reversal.
- A retracement that does not exceed the Open price may result in a reversal from the Open.

---

[2] The veteran day-trader Al Brooks, refers to these types of price action failures with the curious term "Failed failure." Meaning, a possible failure of the market to hold a price level, in this case the support level being tested a third time, has itself failed. Brooks has written a very important trading text for the day-trading community. See Reading Price Charts Bar by Bar, Wiley Trading, 2009 (also noted in the Appendix material).

February 17, 2010. Third-time-down Failure. ES 764-ticks

February 17, 2010. CTs – No Selling Makes for a Poor Short. ES 1-min

Recovering from Failed Trades

A day-trader will experience a large percentage of failed trades. It is common to experience a 25-33% or greater failure rate even from a profitable system. Because day-trading is an exercise in large numbers, the trader must be able to recover psychologically from failed trades. In designing a trading system the mechanics of the system should address the psychology of its practitioners; i.e., Is the system designed so that failed trades do not demoralize the trader?

The e-mini stock index futures system advocated in this book relies on Limit and Stop Market orders placed ahead of the market for both technical and psychological reasons.

Setting orders ahead of the market is preferred because entry is based on pre-defined price levels. Determining a pre-defined price level requires the trader give forethought to setups and helps to eliminate chasing.

Just as important as the technical reasons for using predefined price levels ahead of the market are the psychological ones. If forethought was used to execute an entry order, the trader, even when confronted with a failure, knows that he or she executed a well-defined setup.

I have found this fact helps tremendously with trade psychology. Trade losses are hard to bear, especially when occurring back-to-back, and the trader can quickly lose confidence in him- or herself and in the system traded. Trade losses are doubly hard to bear when generated from Market orders, because then the trader begins to feel that everything is getting away from him – the market is being chased or entry decisions are being made emotionally, even randomly.

Limit and Stop Market orders set ahead of the market promote discipline and with it a positive trading psychology – one feels like a professional involved in a well-defined craft. When Market orders are used that chase, one feels like a gambler. Large winners are possible by jumping on a trend or breakout at just the right moment, but there will also be many losers.

Some traders argue it is a matter of discovering how and when to use Market orders correctly. For example, knowing how to jump on a newly developing change in direction at just the right moment. This may be true. The trading advocated in this book is about trading with a trend or identifying breakouts and reversals, and then entering an order ahead of the market to eliminate chasing.

When a losing trade occurs that has been executed with pre-defined trading rules, the trader can move on to the next trade without feeling chewed up by the market. He has done the job correctly, even if not profitably. In this way, the February 25, 2009 trade described above, which was a small to break even trade, is a winner and adds to a positive trade psychology.

Do Not to Sell Afternoon Rallies Early (or at all)

Every trader has an Achilles Heel and mine is shorting afternoon rallies.

My trading is biased to the short side. This is due to two factors, one objective, the other subjective:

1. When in a winning trade, a short position can give profits immediately. The old adage about market price action – Up like an escalator; Down like an elevator – reinforces the day-trader shorting, as a profitable short position can sometimes be achieved in a matter of minutes or even seconds. Some e-mini futures traders only short the market for this reason.
2. After some reflection, I realize my personality leans toward expecting adversity[3]. I tend to look for, or expect, problems to occur. Looking for sell-offs seems more natural to me, even as I know the overall stock market has a long-term positive bias as it is made up of companies that are growing and attracting investment.

The famous trader Jesse Livermore, immortalized in the classic trading biography Reminiscences of a Stock Operator, by Edwin Lefévre, was said to be a "short plunger" and biased to the short side.

It would be impressive to trade to the long and short sides equally and demonstrate that one is profitable navigating the market in either direction. On the other hand, prevailing market conditions should dictate a long or short bias, even for the short-term day-trader, and this is simply

---

[3] If the reader is taken aback with this kind of introspection, it comes with the territory. If nothing else, trading will teach you about your personality.

good trading. Some traders look at a moving average on daily charts and then only trade intra-day in the same direction as the average. Since the 2008-09 bear market began in earnest back in September 2008, it has been easier to trade to the short side and many intra-day rallies have been marked with rapid and unpredictable sell-offs. This alone can make the trader who is long skittish.

But whatever one's opinion with respect to utilizing both long and short positions, something that must be avoided, is shorting afternoon rallies. Afternoon rallies can generally be classified as one of two types:

1. The rally is unrelenting and continues into the close.
2. The rally is strong but profit-taking occurs in the last hour of the session.

Which ever type of afternoon rally occurs, a system's trade setups must contend with afternoon rallies and adjust accordingly.

March 23, 2009 offered an excellent example. The back-drop to this trading day included:

- The Treasury Department announced a new $1 trillion (!) rescue program for failing U.S. banks, and knowledge of the program was leaked over the weekend and before Monday's open. After several weeks of criticism that the new administration was not adequately addressing the banking issue, the Treasury announcement looked to be positive for Wall Street. ES opened gap-up 19.75 points and did not close the gap in the morning session.
- Before the afternoon session, the Dow was up over 200 points.
- The ES contract first tested the key 800 level (definitely a BN) on March 18th, then retested it the following day, March 19th. The market was poised to break through that key level on its third attempt, which it did convincingly as part of the afternoon rally (ES closed at 818.00).
- CTs were Unequivocally bullish (see chart, below).
- The markets all became IBH RE (Initial Balance High Range Extended).

In summary, it was an enormous rally-day in the stock market. At the close, the Dow finished up 497 points.

Despite all this information, a well-placed YM (Dow) long position was closed with only scalping profits and this was followed by an ill-fated short. The short trade illustrates my trading Achilles Heel and what to avoid when trading the e-mini futures.

The first chart shows the CTs for the day. They are Unequivocally bullish. In fact, by the end of the second hour of trading, just before the lunch hour, the CTs are at the last hour average level, more than three hours ahead of recent positive averages. Along with the other news, an experienced trader should be leery of taking short positions.

The second chart shows a short attempt. There was a well-defined DPH (Day's Previous High) and it was near the 800 BN. Conceivably, the 800 level might hold and could be tested with the DPH. It should have been realized that this was a third test of the 800 level; see the ES 3-minute chart, below. By not paying attention to all the information the market was giving about the strength of the rally (CTs, IBH RE, Lunch-hour buying ledge devoid of selling, etc.) a poor short was attempted.

In summary, with so much bullish information, don't short an afternoon rally, one that picks up steam after the 1:30pm (NYSE) time-of-day pivot. Rather, look to get long after the lunch hour using 3-minute chart 20-EMA retracement or IBH retracement (the ES 3-minute chart, below).

March 23, 2009. Unequivocally Bullish CTs. 1-min chart

Good DPH Retracement Level, BUT

Because of the strong afternoon rally, needed to wait for last hour or last 1/2-hour rally exhaustion

March 23, 2009. Failed DPH Retracement Trade. ES 233-tick

March 23, 2009. Correct Long Entry. ES 3-min

But If You Still Want to Sell Afternoon Rallies . . .

I know as well as anyone the temptation to sell rallies and have lost quite a bit doing so (in my own defense, I haven't actually lost that much account value, because I use tight stops, but I have participated in too many failed short trades during afternoon rallies). The market is high, overbought, and it feels impossible to get in late on a rally, buying high, even as the market just seems to keep going higher and higher. It's frustrating. So the novice looks to the other side: How can I sell this market high?

If you have to sell afternoon rallies, wait until the last hour and carefully watch price action. If there is some "topping" seen – a plateau in the buying (see the March 4th example, below) – and if it is sufficiently late in the session, for example close or into the last half hour of the session (3:30pm Eastern), then it may be possible to get in on a profitable late session sell-off. As always, pay attention to significant price levels and BNs.

If there is rollover late in the session, with a clear trend change as defined by new lows being established, then trying one or two short attempts may make sense. But be forewarned: What looks like an end to an afternoon rally, even late in the session, can be just one more consolidation before another leg up.

The next two charts show a short position in an afternoon rally on March 4, 2009. CTs were Unequivocally bullish, but an end to the rally is seen with the flattened top and a breakout to lower lows into the last half hour of the session. A prudent trader might enter short after the new lower lows and with retracement to the 20-EMA on a tick chart.

March 4, 2009. Afternoon Rally Unequivocal CTs. ES 1-min

March 4, 2009. Breakout to New Lows. ES tick

Is Doubling-Down Ever a Good Idea?

In the Trade Management chapter the Double-Down technique was calculated to improve a vanilla 2-tiered strategy and about equal to the 3-tiered, based on the expected value calculations. However, there may be some cases where the trader can reliably make use of doubling-down based on the strength of a session rally or sell-off.

If the market is seen as Unequivocally bullish or bearish and the goal is to enter in the direction of the trend on a retracement, then doubling-down can sometimes be relied on to eliminate pre-mature entries which would otherwise become losing trades. The high-level view is that the trader is on the correct side of the market, but has made a short-term mistake picking an entry price level. Rather than being stopped out for a loss, the trader trusts his directional call and continues with the trade using a double-down, second entry.

Of course, the double-down can result in a costly loss. What if the market, rather then completing a short-term trend retracement has begun a significant reversal? Then the trader can be caught with a substantial loss. But if the trend is strong, then a retracement is more likely than a reversal and the double-down strategy can work. In addition, if doubling-down is restricted to the early stages of a trend, then the chances may be better that a retracement is occurring and not a reversal[4].

As always, a concrete example helps clarify the pros and cons of a trading technique. The charts from May 19, 2010 give a good one.

Following the May 6, 2010 historic intra-day crash (Dow drops almost 1000 points) there has been increased selling in the stock market, and on May 19th the CTs turn Unequivocally bearish during the morning session. The trader is looking to enter short on a retracement. When the market sells through the Open (1112.75), a patient day-trader might wait for retracement back to the Open for a high probability trade (granted, a Sell Stop Market order just below the Open on the initial breakdown made a very good trade). If the CTs remain bearish, then a retracement to the Open makes a good entry point, and a resting Limit order from the Open minus two ticks (1112.25) is a well-planned trade.

---

[4] The author does not have any back-test data to quantify statements about retracement versus reversal frequency. The most objective measurement of the double-down technique is what was presented with the Trade Management directed graphs.

May 19, 2010. Unequivocally Bearish CTs. ES 1-min

May 19, 2010. Double-Down Trade. ES 3-min

But the trader is also seeing a fairly volatile market and is aware of the approximate two point price discovery phenomenon of the ES contract. Because the CTs are so bearish, the trade will incorporate a double-down at the first entry price plus two points (1114.25). Half the usual number of contracts are used at each entry. In this case, the double-down entry is executed; the market moves one tick above (1114.50), before turning back down.

The three minute ES chart shows the trade. As long as a final stop-loss level (1116.25), here four points above the first entry and two points above the second entry, is defined and maintained, the trade can't be faulted. Note that the final stop-loss was placed above the 1115.00 level (a modest BN) and one tick above 1116.00, so that price would need to break above 1116 to cause a complete trade failure. The Unequivocally bearish CTs and the first retracement back up to the Open supported the use of the double-down technique.

Finally, note that the three minute chart shows another area where this technique could have been used, the later retracement to a double bottom breakdown at the 1105 price level. The two entries, initial and double-down, are shown with the standard small down arrow.

In summary, if the trader is convinced that a strong trend is in-place, for example from reading the CTs or similar indicator, then a double-down strategy from retracement levels may make sense. It is very difficult to estimate the end of a price move, large or small, with too much precision. A carefully designed double-down trade, with pre-set initial and second entries and adherence to a final stop-loss level, may make sense, and can prevent a trade, entered a little too close to the market, from being prematurely stopped out.

Doubling-down on the wrong side of the market and adding to a position that was opened against the trend or a trend reversal, is obviously something that must be avoided. In this regard, the last hour needs to be handled carefully as strong reversals can occur then, often at the beginning of the last hour or thirty minutes into it.

The day-trader will have to experiment with the double-down technique in order to determine a clear set of rules for when to use it and, importantly, to establish the discipline so that it is not over-used. There is one more note about the double-down near the end of this chapter (see the $1M Questions section).

Staying in Trades Following Price Compressions

Compression, consolidation, squeezes – these are terms used to describe periods of non-trending, side-ways price action where the market has temporarily found equilibrium. Neither the bulls nor the bears are able to trade with conviction in order to take the current price higher or lower.

Some technicians purport to draw a correlation to the duration and narrowness of a compression and the strength of a subsequent breakout and price move to a new area of value. The chart from October 21, 2009 shows an extreme case with breakout to the downside. The chart from April 19, 2010 shows somewhat lesser compression followed by a breakout to the upside. One can review price charts and find numerous examples of this phenomenon and there is a rationale to it that draws parallels from nature. Namely, the market is building pressure during a phase of equilibrium for an eventual move to a new value area. The strength of a breakout will be a function of the strength of the original compression.

The bottom line for the day-trader is to stay with a trade that appears to be a breakout from a compression. Sometimes the day-trader will repeatedly scalp, taking a few ticks of profit. Following a compression cycle, it is a shame to scalp out of a trade that is going in one's favor for a few ticks. In this case, make use of the previous compression with the goal of a winning runner. Apply the techniques described in the Trade Management chapter to stay in the trade.

Some clues that will help the trader stay with a breakout are:

- If long and the CTs are showing continuous buying, or if short and the CTs are showing continuous selling (refer to the histogram display), then one can stay with the trade.
- A momentum move from a compression. On a three minute chart, if a wide bullish or bearish candlestick leads the breakout, that can indicate a large move is in the cards.
- If a compression cycle occurs during the noon hour (NYSE, Eastern) and there are signs of an afternoon rally, then the upside can be significant. The trader will have to show patience with afternoon rallies, aware of the adage, "Escalator Up, Elevator Down."

- Breakouts at key price levels; e.g., IBH/L; DPH/L; PDH/L; VAH/L; and inter-day support and resistance, can be the tip-off to large moves.
- Third-time-up/down patterns from ascending/descending triangles can result in large price moves.

In the 4-plex chart from March 11th, 2010 four, almost identical, ascending triangle patterns with third time up breakouts are shown. Here is an example of where scalping out of a successful long position from the breakout would have left much on the table. The trader should let the long compression period prior to the breakout work for him. The fact that all four e-mini stock index futures gave such strikingly similar price action might have indicated there would be significant upside.

There are many technical indicators that can help the trader identify compression cycles. The well-known Bollinger Band within Keltner Band study and the APR indicator described in the Trading Basics chapter are two examples. But often, the trader can simply eye-ball three minute price charts, or the equivalent, in order to identify compressions.

October 21, 2009. Compression to Bear Breakout. ES 3-min

April 19, 2010. Compression to Bull Breakout. ES 3-min

March 11, 2010. Compression to Bull Breakout. E-mini 4-plex (simplified)

Buy Low, Sell High

We hear the "Buy Low, Sell High" mantra continually. In fact, it is the first rule of trading – on any time frame and with any setup – and it can refer to absolute price levels as well as local retracements. Some examples:

- Buy the PDL, DPL, IBL; Sell the PDH, DPH, IBH.
- Buy a retracement down to the 20-EMA on a trend up; Sell a retracement up to the 20-EMA on a trend down.
- Buy an upside breakout pullback; Sell a downside breakout pullback.

Stop Market orders were not advocated in the 1st Edition of this book because they do not follow the Buy Low, Sell High rule. If the market is not suitably trending, they can cause the trader to get caught in breakout head fakes, buying high and selling low[5].

If one steps back and looks at the trading day as a whole, it is straightforward to see the best Buy Low, Sell High opportunities in a session. Of course, it's much harder to do this in real-time as the trading day unfolds. If the trader applies some patience, and waits for enough of the day's price architecture to be established, then it may be possible to place good Buy Low, Sell High trades. Sometimes these trades can be held for long periods of time and realize significant winning runners, because they have been set at the day's extrema (high or low).

Some day-traders practice intra-day swing trades and scalps simultaneously, and even on the same contract using multiple accounts. In one account, there might be a long intra-day swing position taken in the ES contract, while scalping the NQ contract to the short side. Generally, the swing position is making use of perceived intra-day highs or lows and may remain open with a relatively small number of contracts using wider stops; or the swing trade is in a no-lose position following profit-taking from some number of fast exit contracts.

The three minute NQ chart from March 15, 2010 illustrates a Buy Low/Sell High swing trade mentality. Here, the trader patiently watches the market long enough to believe the intra-day lows have been tested and a consolidation base can be traded before a possible upside move.

---

[5] The reader is encouraged to review the Price Pattern setups and come to his or her own conclusion as to the right mix of Limit and Stop Market trade entries to use.

After a series of tests, for example double bottoms hold, the trader realizes that for a few points of risk, he may be able to enter at the day's lows. The trader executes with a smaller number of contracts than might normally be used, does not scalp profits, and simply holds the position, almost as if in the background, for much of the remainder of the day.

The trader can make use of the CTs, or similar indicator, to review overall stock market activity looking for technical support for this kind of intra-day swing position. The CTs chart from March 15th, below, gives an example. If the buying ledge continues to hold, then a review of the CTs confirms the market stabilizing without further large selling spikes in the NYSE Ticks. Earlier, the CTs, though bearish, were not Unequivocal, and this might have been used in the decision to test what was perceived as the day's low.

One can argue that this trading style also puts in practice high probability trading, as the position risks a small number of points while being held open for a possible large move off what may be the day's extrema. The trading mentality is to "let the market prove me wrong" and the trader disciplines himself to hold off scalping and leave the position alone.

Having the patience to wait for the consolidation buying/selling ledge to form helps the trader both define a suitable stop-loss level as well as stay in the trade. If the area of consolidation is at a BN, or previous support/resistance level, the trade setup can be more compelling.

On March 26, 2010 there was a definite topping pattern to the ES contract. Furthermore, the CTs were very flat and Equivocal, not indicating a trend up at this point. Here a two point stop-loss was traded for the opportunity to short from near the day's highs. I have made these kinds of trades with very small numbers of contracts (even single e-minis) with the goal of holding on for much of the day, realizing a two point loss is only $100 in the ES, while the gain, trading from what could be the day's extrema, might be substantial.

Note that in the March 26th trade, a short would not be taken if there was an indication that we might trend higher. The combination of flat CTs combined with a shorting ledge made for a high probability trade.

March 15, 2010. Buying Low and Holding On. NQ 3-min

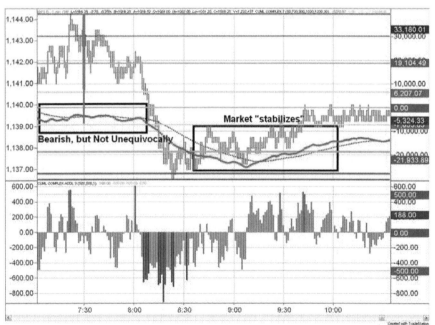

March 15, 2010. CTs Favor a Buying Decision. ES 1-min

March 26, 2010. Selling High from a Shorting Ledge. ES 3-min

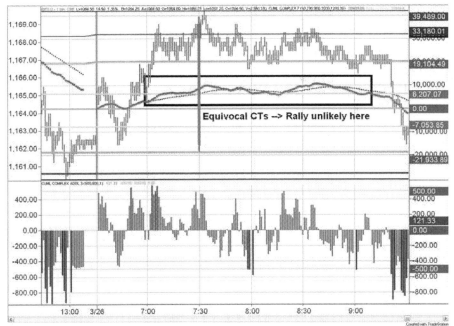

March 26, 2010. CTs Favor a Short Decision. ES 1-min

The Use of 24hr Globex Prices in the Day Session

The trading in this book is focused on the day session, 9:30am to 4:15pm Eastern (NYSE). As described in the introduction to the e-minis, the CME Globex trades almost 24 hours a day, with short daily maintenance downtimes and a weekend break following Friday's NYSE close. Globex trading proceeds around the clock and globe.

In the overnight session, volumes are typically very light relative to the day session, unless a serious and unexpected overnight news event occurs. There can be increased trading volume in the hour before the stock market opens (8:30am, Eastern), if an unexpected economic report result is released ahead of the open.

Generally, the day-trader does not concern himself with Globex overnight trading[6], however, he should generally be aware of overnight session highs and lows in the ES contract (the other contracts are too lightly traded to be reviewed) as they give price levels to watch or take advantage of during the day session.

The ES chart[7] below, from the middle of April 2010, shows the 24-hour contract above the day session chart. Referring to the 24-hour bar chart, we see that support was maintained at the 1202 level (=1200 BN + 2) during two over-night sessions, and so the 1202 Globex support level further reinforces an appreciation of the 1200 level being key. In this regard, if the market breaks convincingly below 1200, then there could be significant further downside, which is what in fact occurred.

Day-traders may want to use Globex 24hr highs and lows as price levels to fade with Equivocal CTs or to watch for breakout trades, with Stop Market orders or Breakout Pullback (BOP) entries.

---

[6] Mechanical systems implementers are always asking whether their moving average and other indicators should include or ignore the overnight activity.
[7] Trading desktops typically distinguish between the day and 24-hour session using symbol prefixes/suffixes. @ES.D is the day session continuous ES contract and @ES is the 24-hour continuous contract on TradeStation.

April 2010. Globex 24-hour contract. ES 30-min

The Importance of Key Price Levels Can't be Over-looked

Trading the e-mini stock index futures everyday, one becomes impressed with the way key price levels act as support and resistance. For the retail trader far removed from any inside information of how large funds and institutions actively trade[8], the only explanation is that the large participants, and the increasingly prevalent high-frequency automation, use stock index and stock index futures price levels to make trading decisions about individual stocks. In this way, there is a feedback loop between the buying and selling of individual stocks and the movement of the stock market derivatives.

For example, if a fund needs to sell a large block of IBM, then it will want to do so at local retracement peaks throughout the day. If ES futures have just fallen below 1050, as an example, then a retracement back to the 1050 level could be used by the professional to sell more IBM shares. And in the realm of high-frequency automated trading, which may be the new norm, computers are programmed to execute orders based on pre-defined price levels and price extensions and retracements. Similar arguments apply to well-known intrinsic price levels; e.g., the Open, IBH/L, PDH/L, etc. In this way, the stock market and stock index and stock index futures play off each other.

While there is no back-test data offered at this point to substantiate claims made about key price levels[9], the discretionary trader is used to seeing too much predictable trading around key price levels to ignore them. Their use can make for well-defined and pre-determined trade entries ahead of the market, which reduce the temptation to chase.

From April 23, 2010, the ES market tests the IBL by one tick before moving more than 12 points higher. The IBL was at 1201.25 just five ticks above the very Big Number 1200.

From April 26, 2010, the IBL holds as the day's low (DPL) up until the last hour. Once the IBL/DPL level is broken, the market moves down some

---

[8] Spending time on the floor at the CME and CBOE, and visiting with NYSE specialists, didn't bring any insights as to the way in which institutions trade. Or it was the case that no one in the know was willing to let me in on their secrets; probably the latter.

[9] It could be the case that the discretionary trader is just being fooled by a phenomenon whereby the mind attempts to bring order and repeatability to an otherwise random price chart. See the Aronson text referenced earlier.

four points testing new lows on the day. When a price level remains the day's high/low for a significant period of the day, with repeated tests at those levels, then breakouts to new highs/lows on the day can create good trading opportunities (3TU, 3TD, BOP price patterns).

From May 18, 2010, the ES contract range extends the IBL (IBL RE) shortly after the IB has formed. A retracement move takes the market to within two ticks of the IBL before continuing lower.

From May 19, 2010, the ES contract tests the 1100.00 price level by five ticks and then executes a sharp 'V' reversal. 1100 is obviously a very Big Number (BN) for the contract (and the two point discovery phenomenon may have applied here, as well).

From May 20, 2010, the ES contract opens gap down, moves significantly below its open and then retraces to just three ticks above the open before making an almost 20 point move lower. Later in the same session, the contract retraces to within one tick of the day's previous high (DPH) before making a final push down of over 25 points.

From May 21, 2010, after overnight selling has the ES contract opening gap down, the market tests the Previous Day's Low (PDL) twice, by one and three ticks, each time finding support.

Rather than bore the reader with more examples, he or she is encouraged to review price charts to see if a case can be made for the importance of key price levels. Trades made around price levels can make for well-defined setups. Trades where initial stop-loss can be set just outside of key price levels represent low-risk entries.

April 23, 2010. IBL Tested. ES 3-min

April 26, 2010. IBL Range Extension. ES 3-min

May 18, 2010. IBL Retracement. ES 3-min

May 19, 2010. 1100 BN Holds. ES 3-min

May 20, 2010. Open and DPH Retracements. ES 3-min

May 21, 2010. PDL Holds. ES 3-min

$1M Questions Every Day-Trader Must Answer

Here are four "Million Dollar" questions that the active trader must answer every day. Being able to supply detailed answers to these questions, including specific instructions that can be used in practice, indicates one is moving beyond the level of novice trader[10].

Of course, there are many other equally relevant questions. These four are some of the best and most important I know of for the day-trader.

The questions are posed first, without any answers, so that the reader can consider and provide his or her own responses. Detailed answers, derived from the material in this book, are on the next page.

1. Is an immediate retracement to a breakout level a breakout pullback, to be traded in the direction of the breakout, or is the breakout going to fail (a head-fake)?

2. In a trending market, is the most recent retracement to the EMA the beginning of a trend reversal or a retracement that can be used to get on the trend?

3. Should one exit a positive position with a profit target scalp or use a trailing stop for a longer-term winning runner?

4. Having faded the market at one price level, and with the trade failing, should one double-down (DD) from a new price level (with wider final stop-loss) or just stay put?

---

[10] See <u>Mind over Markets</u>, John Dalton, Eric Jones, and Robert Dalton, Traders Press, Inc., 1993, for a good description of a trader's evolution from beginner to expert.

1. Is an immediate retracement to a breakout level a breakout pullback, to be traded in the direction of the breakout, or is the breakout going to fail (a head-fake)?

   A true breakout can be distinguished from a false breakout based on:

   - If EMA' (EMA rate-of-change) is in the direction of the breakout, then it may be a true breakout. A meandering EMA often indicates lack of conviction in price, which can lead to false breakouts. For example, a clearly negative EMA' off recent highs that is above a 3TD level supports a true downside breakout. In this case, price action corresponds closely to a descending triangle pattern and not a sideways market.
   - If there is "air" above or below the breakout level, then it may improve the chances of a breakout. Air above/below means we are buying low or selling high with the breakout. For example, 3TU breakouts from the day's highs or 3TD breakouts from the day's lows are more likely to fail, in general.
   - If the CTs are aligned with the breakout, then it may result in a true breakout. For example, a 3TD breakout against a CTs histogram that has shown no selling probably indicates a head-fake and not a true breakout.

2. In a trending market, is the most recent retracement to the EMA the beginning of a trend reversal or a retracement that can be used to get on the trend?

   Trend retracement versus trend reversal can be distinguished using the following techniques:

   - If the EMA' is still strongly in the direction of the trend, then we probably won't yet see a reversal. An EMA' that is approaching zero indicates a possible trend change. Retracements that occur later in a trend are less reliable retracements for getting on the trend than those in the first half of a trend.
   - If there have been Unequivocal CTs and now, as part of the retracement the CTs are not showing strength in the direction of the retracement – for example, they are flat –

then we most likely are seeing a retracement and not a reversal. This can be a CTs-Price Divergence indicating retracement, with trend continuation to follow, as opposed to a reversal.

- If the MACD has rotated from OB to OS or OS to OB, then we may have an exhausted trend and the retracement cannot be relied on.
- RHS patterns should be used to test a possible reversal with long entries. PDT and 3TF patterns should be used to test a possible reversal with short entries.

3. Should one exit a positive position with a profit target scalp or use a trailing stop for a longer-term winning runner?

The following rules can be applied, listed in highest-to-lowest priority order:

- If CTs are Unequivocal and the trade is in the direction of the day's trend, then stay in the position.
- If recent CTs are 100% consistent with the position (long → only positive CTs histogram bars; short → only negative CTs histogram bars), then stay in the position.
- If the trade follows a period of congestion, then stay in the position.
- If tick chart candlesticks are increasing in frequency and showing almost no adverse bars (long → mostly green; short → mostly red), then stay in the position.
- If the MACD has not rotated to new OB/OS levels, then stay in the position.

4. Having faded the market at one price level, and with the trade failing, should one double-down (DD) from a new price level (with wider final stop-loss) or just stay put?

There are two cases where doubling-down can be justified:

- If the trade is a retracement entry used to enter with the trend, and it is believed the initial entry was simply placed too close to the market, then a DD second entry can be justified. This style of trading was described earlier in the chapter. A DD can be supported if trading with Unequivocal CTs, for example. Final stop-loss must be used, in any case, and should not be repeatedly moved to prevent staying with a DD when a trend reversal may be occurring. A DD that is on the wrong side of the market will result in a significant loss. CTs-Price Divergence can indicate retracements which may warrant a DD second entry.

- If the trade is pre-planned around BNs or well-defined price levels (e.g., PDH, Open, etc.), then a DD second entry can be justified. In this case, the DD entry is planned as part of the original trade setup – it was not an afterthought. The trader should write down the exact first, DD and stop-loss levels he will be using ahead of the trade and all entries should be resting Limit orders. Also, it is a good idea to use one-half the usual number of contracts at each level, so that if the DD occurs, the trader has his typical allotment of contracts in the position.

    Example: Short ES from 1199.50. DD from 1201.50. Final exit at 1203.00. Here the huge BN 1200 is used to fade the market. Make sure that the fade is not on a 3TU attempt and that the trade is not against Unequivocal CTs (here, bullish). Also, the final stop-loss level should be outside the BN +/- 2 point area. Here it was 1203.00, one point above 1202.00.

A Trading Playbook

If the reader has made it this far, then the sentiment, "Too much information and too much detail – I don't know how to trade it," is valid. The book has covered many market views, many trade setups, and many strategies. It may be unclear how to put it all together and trade.

On the other hand, it is unrealistic to expect that a system can be quickly purchased or learned, and then used to make easy money. The world simply isn't going to give us a living so effortlessly.

A common problem with acquiring a system becomes apparent soon after beginning to use it. When losing trades occur, which they undoubtedly will, and the user does not have an understanding of the system's logic or has not invested in its development, then everything is quickly called into question. It's human nature when valuable capital is put on the line. I have purchased best-of-class mechanical systems and executed them to spec or had a CTA/IB execute them for me. But when too many back-to-back losers occurred, I threw in the towel, even when I began the program with a promise to stay with it.

I believe one has to develop unique, individual trading systems over time and from the experience of actually trading. This book is meant to facilitate the development of such personalized trading[11].

In any case, we still haven't addressed the issue at hand – Help putting the book's material together in a cohesive program so that trading can begin. Here is one technique for doing so.

What is needed is to assemble a trading *playbook*. The playbook is built over time and based on individual trading experience and personal preference.

Here is one example playbook. There are obviously an unlimited number of playbooks that can be developed, because we are in effect back to

---

[11] Because there are some very good CTAs and money managers in the industry, an alternative to this is for the trader-investor to perform extensive due diligence, becoming familiar with a CTA/manager and his or her track record and trading system; and then rely on the individual as opposed to a black box. However, this is an entirely different proposition to trading one's own account.

defining trade strategy. However, here we are doing so in the context of the material presented in the text.

This playbook example covers the following areas, because experience shows that these techniques make for high probability trades:

- A small set of price patterns which take advantage of the market's tendency to sharply sell-off.
- Use of an IMD (Inter-Market Divergence) setup, because experience shows they can be relatively straightforward to identify and often create good winning runner possibilities.
- Participation in rallies, both to offset the short-side mentality of the first technique and because whatever the general market conditions, there are strong intra-day rallies. If a buying ledge develops, it can make for a low-risk/high-return trade (stop-loss set just outside the ledge).

Having set the objectives for the playbook, it's now possible to assemble the details. The table below summarizes the example. It consists of three well-defined trades. There are an unlimited number of variations, but the goal is for the trader to stick to the playbook, developing and modifying it slowly over time based on his or her profitability and experience.

A missing component may be the ability to quantify a playbook in order to help make decisions about adding or subtracting setups. Keeping careful records of which trade types, time-of-day usage, scalping versus longer-term winning runners, etc., are most profitable will definitely help going forward.

Another alternative is to take an automation and back-test approach, testing strategies against historical market data. This re-opens the larger question of discretionary versus mechanical system trading.

The equity curve below tests a new playbook entry based on IB RE and CTs pivot values. It shows a three year equity curve using one ES contract. Initial stop-loss and profit-target are fixed at approximately 1% of contract value. It is impressive that the strategy did well during both the 2008 sell-off and the 2009 reversal rally. Perhaps this is the next stage in the development of an e-mini day-trading program – a back-test assessment of playbook setups.

Description	Setup Details and Notes
3TD SHORT (Third Time Down)	▪ CTs not bullish or have moved from bullish to flat ▪ Trade off the day's highs – lower probability when trading to new lows ▪ Don't trade when 20-EMA is flat, which can lead to third-time-down failure head-fakes ▪ Initial stop-loss above 20-EMA or most recent swing high ▪ Breakout trade amenable to scalping ▪ BOP SHORT can be used to add to a position
IMD + IB RE (Inter-Market Divergence plus IB Range Extension)	▪ Leader market has IB RE before a follower ▪ Enter the extension in the follower market using a Stop Market order 1-2 ticks outside the IB ▪ An alternative entry follows the IB RE with a retracement entry at the IBL/H. BOP or EMA retracement entries. This can be used if the breakout is initially missed
PM LONG WITH CTs FROM LEDGE (PM rally from low-risk entry)	▪ AM session and/or noon-hour consolidation ▪ Consolidation following bullish CTs ▪ Can use IMD designation, picking a laggard ▪ Long entry with stop-loss just below well-defined buying ledge; RHS LONG may be used ▪ Move to no-lose position and attempt to hold a winning runner

Example Trade Playbook

Equity Curve Line - @ES.D 1 min.(05/29/07 06:31 - 05/28/10 13:15)

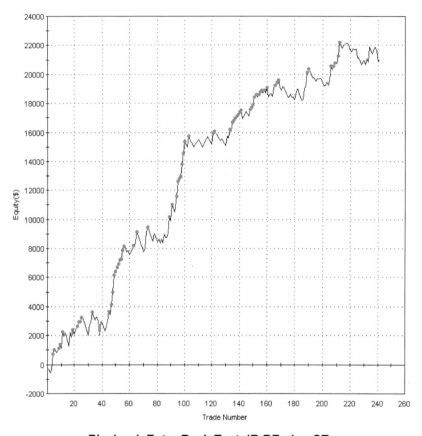

Playbook Entry Back-Test: IB RE plus CTs.
3-Year Equity Curve. One ES contract.
40% Annual Rate of Return on $10K/CAR Initial Capital.

Final Thoughts

There is no single technique that offers success in the very difficult task of day-trading the e-mini futures market. Rather, it has been my goal to describe methods that anticipate the market and make use of efficient trade management to create a trading system that produces positive expected value.

An individual trader competes against participants who are applying many of the same techniques and tools on the other side of his or her trades. Developing personal confidence and discipline can make or break the prospective trader. Experience counts more than any specific technique.

I continue to have losing days and believe they are unavoidable. When looking back at failed trades I realize they are the result of not following rules – making mistakes that could be avoided, and over-trading in a desire to make easy money. But I am also convinced that if anticipation is used with accurate stop-loss and profit-targets, then profitability can be achieved.

The prospective trader will need to practice and convince himself of this. The beginner should plan on making hundreds, even thousands, of trades, using a small number of contracts and sufficiently tight stop-loss (from the Trade Management chapter, keep $x=1$ initially). Success begets success and gives the confidence needed to continue trading. Obviously, if it were easy, and profitability could be realized automatically, we wouldn't be trading an actual market. The market does not offer a free lunch.

As with any non-trivial endeavor, education is vital. I have paid for individual mentoring and for memberships in internet trading rooms. This education has been important, even if expensive, in some cases costing several thousands of dollars or more. Trade education is important, but be aware that there is no trading Holy Grail to miraculously uncover.

More important than specific trade setups and techniques is the discipline needed to follow a trading program. This is only attained through personal trial and error. Here, again, the most important ingredient, above all, is experience. I am leery of trade educators offering success.

I am even more leery of students of trade educators who pronounce that they have been quickly and regularly profitable after participating in a trading course. There is a strong desire to claim success in this.

I wrote this book as much for my own development as a trader as to describe what I believe to be good trading techniques. The book is offered at a modest price to recoup some of the time and energy it has taken me to write it. It is not meant to describe a guaranteed road to success. There really is no such thing.

I am not trying to initiate a trading education enterprise with this book. I believe traders must ultimately build unique, individualized systems, slowly over time. The best outcome would be for the reader to study the book and then, after some experimentation, incorporate what he or she finds to be the best aspects of the system in their trading. To this end, the indicators and charts I use are available online, also at a nominal price. See the Appendix for how to purchase these.

§§§

Trading System Two-Page Summary

The e-mini stock index futures day-trading system described in this book makes use of **Day-Type, Price Level, Technical Indicator, Time-of-Day and Price Pattern** to define trade setups:

- Determine the day-type and trade with it. The CTs indicator is a useful tool to help the trader determine the day-type. Don't fade a trending market. Don't trade on the wrong side of an afternoon rally. Strong trends (Unequivocal CTs) can be entered using a 3-min, 20-EMA retracement in the direction of the trend.

- Anticipate the market at key price levels. Enter trades with orders placed ahead of the market at small offsets from key price levels (Initial Balance High/Low, Day's Previous High/Low; Previous Day's High/Low; Open, recent support and resistance). When Inter-Market Price Divergences are discernable – price level discrepancies between the four key e-mini stock index futures (ES, TF, NQ, YM) – additional trading opportunities exist.

- Make use of a small set of technical indicators to gauge market direction and price extension. Trading in the direction of the 20-EMA and MACD improve the probability of a successful trade. If price extension occurs at a key price level and in a non-trending market, then reversal trades can be profitable. If a reversal fails, automated fast-exit and stop-loss execution will minimize losses.

- Pay attention to time-of-day. Wait for time-of-day pivots against which to trade (first half-hour; IB; long entries after lunchtime consolidation and before the afternoon rally pivot; last hour and last half-hour reversal pivots). The post-lunch, early afternoon can be the most difficult time to be short. Don't get caught early on the wrong side of an afternoon rally.

- Enter the market with a price pattern. Have a well-defined set of price patterns that are used to enter trades and trade with them. Find a small set of patterns with which you have confidence and repeatedly follow them.

The system uses well-defined **Trade Management** to enter and exit trades:

- <u>Enter the market with pre-defined limit or stop market orders</u>. Do not chase with market orders. All trade entries should be set ahead of market price action.

- <u>Apply expected value trade management calculations</u>. Define and use stop-loss and profit-target objectives. Don't use wide stops. Determine a realistic strategy and then program automated order entry software (e.g., NinjaTrader) to execute trades.

- <u>A successful trade has a high winning percentage and fixed profit-target or quickly moves to a no-lose position with the chance of a winning runner</u>. Incorporate a technical indicator to add trailing stops to a winning runner position. Adjust trailing stops based on price action and day-type.

Thank You and Good Luck!

Thank you for reading my (second) contribution to the fascinating endeavor of trading the e-mini stock index futures.

I wish you the best in trading or on whatever path your career takes you!

Michael Gutmann
Hillsboro, Oregon
Spring 2010

Appendices

Appendix I: Investing and Trading Reading – Short List

Market Wizards, Jack Schwager, HarperBusiness, 1993. The first book I would read. (GENERAL)

Reminiscences of a Stock Operator, Edwin Lefevre, John Wiley & Sons, Inc., 1994. The book everyone says is a must read. The story of Jesse Livermore considered one of the greatest traders ever. (GENERAL)

Pit Bull, Martin Schwartz, HarperBusiness, 1998. Very entertaining. Fun way to start reading about traders. (GENERAL, FUTURES)

HedgeHogging, Barton Biggs, John Wiley & Sons, 2006. A much talked about book by a well-known, highly experienced, Wall-Streeter. Fascinating look at the hedge fund industry. Entertaining. (GENERAL)

Intermarket Analysis, John Murphy, John Wiley & Sons, 2004. An overview of the broader financial markets. Nothing here to trade or invest, but it gives one a view of the bigger picture. (GENERAL)

Stock Traders Almanac, Yale Hirsch and Jeffrey Hirsch, John Wiley & Sons. Note: It's updated and printed yearly. I have the 2004 edition. Any recent year will do. Good overview of some fundamental and technical patterns seen in stocks. (STOCKS)

Martin Zweig's Winning on Wall Street, Martin Zweig, Warner Books, 1986. Kind of a classic; Zweig is well-respected. Shows a number of the Hirsch trends in more detail. (STOCKS)

How to Make Money in Stocks, William O'Neil, McGraw-Hill, 2002. William O'Neil made a fortune trading in the 1960s-1980s and is a legendary trader. He began Investors Business Daily to compete with the Wall Street Journal. (Take a look at a free trial subscription at www.investors.com.) He's noted for something called CANSLIM, a fundamental stock picking strategy. His fundamental analysis is good. I'm not so sure about his heavy reliance on the cup-and-handle technical entry. He always advocated long positions for the small, retail investor, even as some of his personal best trades were shorts. He's since come out with a book that gives short strategies. I haven't read it. (STOCKS)

Mind over Markets, John Dalton, Eric Jones, and Robert Dalton, Traders Press, Inc., 1993. A good introduction to J. Peter Steidlmayer's techniques. Steidlmayer is a legendary futures trader and has developed some of the best theory, referred to as "The Market Profile," for looking at markets. Linda Bradford Raschke (Market Wizards fame; outstanding trade practitioner) says this book is a must read. (FUTURES)

Options on Futures, John Summa and Jonathan Lubow, John Wiley & Sons, 2002. A good, gentle introduction to futures and futures options. Be careful of the options writing/premium strategies. (FUTURES, OPTIONS)

Option Volatility and Pricing, Sheldon Natenberg, McGraw-Hill, 1994. When I visited the CBOE in 2003, two different traders asked me, "Have you read Natenberg?" When I answered, "No," they replied, "Well, you need to, because the guy on the other side of your trade has." I've read this book three times now. It is quite technical, but note that a true quant considers it elementary – to give you an idea of the sophistication of the derivatives market. (OPTIONS)

Mastering the Trade, John Carter, McGraw-Hill, 2006. Carter is one of the better retail traders out there. The book gives a good idea of how contemporary traders, day and swing, operate. (STOCKS, FUTURES, OPTIONS)

Trading Systems and Methods, Perry J. Kaufman, John Wiley & Sons, Third Edition, 1998. Top-notch, in-depth review of trading technicals. Extraordinarily comprehensive. (STOCKS, FUTURES)

Reading Price Charts Bar by Bar: The Technical Analysis of Price Action for the Serious Trader, Al Books, Wiley Trading, 2009. This is a very important book. Al Brooks has been day-trading for some 20 years and brings an uncommon insight and intelligence to the endeavor. The book is dense and it can be exhausting to follow all the bar-by-bar discussion, but it is a book every day-trader should read. (STOCKS, FUTURES, DAY-TRADING)

Appendix II: Author references and purchasing trading software used in the book

The author can be reached at: michaeljgutmann@gmail.com.

The software used by the trading system, TradeStation EasyLanguage routines and workspaces, and Excel spreadsheets, can be purchased at: www.anticipationtrading.com.

The TradeStation desktop is available at: www.tradestation.com.

NinjaTrader software is available at: www.ninjatrader.com.

Invivo.Stops software is available at: www.invivoanalytics.com.

§§§

Index

About the author

For 20 years Michael Gutmann was a software engineer and manager at Intel Corporation. He is the co-author of 10 patents in areas of video conferencing, digital video and computer architecture technology, and has Math and Computer Science degrees from the Institute of Technology, University of Minnesota. Mr. Gutmann trades his system daily and publishes in the trade press, writing about retail electronic futures trading. He can be reached at michaeljgutmann@gmail.com.

11469561R0019

Made in the USA
Lexington, KY
06 October 2011